The Church

RUSSELL P. SPITTLER

GOSPEL PUBLISHING HOUSE
SPRINGFIELD, MISSOURI
02-0910

THE CHURCH
© 1977 by the Gospel Publishing House, Springfield, Missouri 65802. All rights reserved. This book is adapted from *The Church,* a manual in the Christian Faith Series and written by Russell P. Spittler, © 1963 by the Gospel Publishing House.

ISBN 0-88243-910-3
Library of Congress Catalog Card Number 77-83982
Printed in the United States of America

A teacher's guide for group study with this book is available from the Gospel Publishing House (order number 32-0180).

Foreword

Everywhere in the world you find the Christian Church. A towering Gothic cathedral in Europe. A quaint, white-frame building nestled in a quiet New England town. A large, square tabernacle in a busy metropolis. A Salvation Army mission on some skid row. A gathering of black faces in the African bush. Uniformed sailors hearing their chaplain on the high seas—here is the Church.

But what is the Church? Is it a building? a religious service? an institution? a congregation? a denomination? Yes, it is all these. But it is something more. It is the body of the Lord Jesus Christ, of which He is the divinely appointed Head. The Head rules in heaven from the right hand of the Father. The Body works on earth, the footstool of the Father.

If you are a Christian, you belong to this Body. You are a stone in God's building, a plant on God's farm, a sheep in God's pasture. You have brothers and sisters "in the Lord" whom you may never see till the great day of assembly in heaven. All of you make up the Body.

You, your brothers and sisters before you, did things for God. You evangelized. You defended the faith. You suffered persecutions. Once, you became wealthy and influential at the high cost of spiritual decay. Some of you brought about reform. Others of you reestablished the missionary enterprise. This is the history of the Church—your history.

This small book traces the theology and the history of the church of Jesus Christ. May God grant us all spiritual vision so we may never be guilty of "not discerning the Lord's body" (1 Corinthians 11:29).

Contents

1 Origin of the Church 7

2 Nature of the Church 16

3 Scope of the Church 25

4 Message of the Church 35

5 The Lord's Supper 44

6 Water Baptism 51

7 Organization of the Church 59

8 Destiny of the Church 68

9 The Early Church 76

10 The Medieval Church 86

11 The Reformation 95

12 The Early Modern Church 106

13 The Twentieth Century 116

Suggestions for Further Reading 126

1

Origin of the Church

Deep in the personal and loving heart of God lies His desire for fellowship. To satisfy this longing He created man. The overarching purpose of man is to glorify God by entering into voluntary fellowship with Him.

We all know that God's original creation of man was marred through Adam's disobedience. It was necessary for God to create man with the inner ability to disobey Him; otherwise, man would have been a mere machine. He would have glorified God automatically, just as the "heavens" and the "firmament" do (Psalm 19:1).

Yet the loving heart of God bent further, to provide a sacrifice in the form of His own Son, thereby opening the way to fellowship.

All who have accepted the Son, who have believed in Jesus, have become members of "the church, which is his body" (Ephesians 1:22, 23). This Church is the fellowship of the redeemed, the people of God, the society of God. It consists of all those in every place and in all ages who by faith have been placed into vital, living union with the Head of the Church—Jesus Christ.

How *the* Church Began

The English word *church* has a number of meanings. A church is (1) a building in which people worship. It may be (2) an actual service of worship. Sometimes the church is viewed as (3) an institution, as opposed, for example, to the state. Or, it may mean (4) a denomination.

But in the New Testament the word for church is not used in these senses. Instead it applies to the local group of believers who customarily worship in one place (1 Corinthians 1:2; Philemon 2), or the entire group of all Christians viewed as existing at a given time (1 Corinthians 12:28) or viewed as including all the redeemed in the past, present, and future (Ephesians 1:22).

1. *Planned and foretold by the Father.* To reach the real origin of the Church, we must—as suggested earlier—go back to the mind and heart of God the Father. For it was God himself who created the people of whom the Church is made up. Tucked away in 1 Corinthians 10:31 is the whole purpose of man: "Whatsoever ye do, do all to the glory of God."

So the Church strikes its roots as far back as the purposes of God. The Church is that group which, like none other, glorifies God and carries out His will on earth.

When actually did the Church originate? The Christian Church has generally dated itself from the Day of Pentecost, when believers received an unprecedented fullness of the Spirit of God and scaled a new height in intimate fellowship with the triune God.

Strictly speaking, the Church is a New Testament idea and institution. Check an exhaustive concordance and you will discover that the word *church,* which appears 112 times in the New Testament, does not appear in the Old Testament. Does this mean there was no Church in the Old Testament? Certainly the institution which Jesus spoke of in the future tense ("I *will* build my church") did not then exist. But if we expand our notion of the Church to define it as the *people of God,* we shall understand that God has always had a Church. Furthermore, Stephen spoke about "the church in the wilderness" when he referred to the Children of Israel under Moses (Acts 7:38).

God has always had a people, even when Elijah thought he was the only one left (1 Kings 19:10, 18). In the Old Testament, this people is called the congregation; while in the New Testament they are found in the Church.

In the Church, therefore, we reach the organization (organism) of men embodying the highest possible fellowship with God. For this age, ever since the fulfilled promise of Jesus, God's people are found in the Church. And by virtue of the available fullness of God's Spirit, they are more truly God's people than was ever possible under the religion of bulls and goats.

In the sweep of history, God has come closer and closer to man. It was in "the fullness of the time" that His Son came to earth (Galatians 4:4). There was a time when the possibility of everyone experiencing God's Spirit was only a wish (Numbers 11:29). Then Joel, speaking by the word of the Lord, converted this wish into a divine promise (Joel 2:28). Next, Peter reported that Joel's promise had become reality (Acts 2:16). And the same apostle left open the same experience "unto you, and to your children, and to all that are afar off" (v. 39). It has not always been possible for every believer to be filled with the Spirit of God.

Along with the increasing intimacy between God and man, actually in direct relation to it, the emergence of the Church must be understood. Speaking through the prophet Jeremiah, God foretold the arrival of days when the Law He had written on stone would be written on hearts (Jeremiah 31:31-34). That this promise stands fulfilled, at least in part in the ministry of Christ as the Head of the Church, is clear in Hebrews 8 and 9 (see especially 8:6; 9:15).

Similarly, the apostle Paul discusses the Church—including as it does both Jew and Gentile—in terms of a "mystery, which from the beginning of the world hath been hid in God." A mystery "which in other ages was not made known unto the sons of men, as it is now revealed unto his holy apostles and prophets by the Spirit" (Ephesians 3:5, 9).

2. *Purchased and founded by the Son.* Note again that the Trinity has participated in the formation of the Church. While the Father originated the plans for the Church, it is the Son who actually built the Church. Using the building analogy, you might say that the Father is the Architect, the Son is the Contractor, and the Spirit is the Operator or Administrator.

Jesus Christ founded the Church. He did so, however, more by what He did than by what He said. What did Jesus have to say about the Church? Surprisingly, He said very little. In all we have recorded of the words of Jesus, He spoke of the Church on only two occasions. (In fact, the word *church* appears in the Gospels only three times, all in Matthew.) The first time He spoke of the Church was on the occasion of Peter's confession (Matthew 16:18). The other instance was Jesus' instructions about an offending brother (18:17). These two are the only places where Jesus speaks directly about the Church.

Jesus talked far more about the *kingdom of God*. This phrase appears again and again in the Gospels and is one of the commonest expressions of Jesus. It seems that by the phrase "kingdom of God" Jesus referred to the total rule of God, even over those who do not obey that rule. The phrase can be translated the "reign of God" or the "sway of God."

In the familiar passage of Matthew 16:13-18, Jesus promises to build His church "upon this rock." In this passage the Greek words for "Peter" and "rock" are about as close as are "save" and "savior" in English. If Jesus spoke Aramaic, the words would have been one and the same. On this basis the Roman Catholic Church has interpreted this passage to give Peter himself some sort of definite priority and supremacy over all the other apostles. From that conclusion ultimately has developed the idea of infallible popes.

Who or what is the "rock" on which Jesus proceeded to build His church? The "rock" is generally viewed by Protestants as Peter's declaration of faith as he spoke for the apostolic band and discerned the true identity of Jesus. By "on this rock," Jesus meant, "On the solid foundation of faith in me will I erect My edifice of the people of God." By His careful teaching and example, Jesus had developed the faith of this unlikely band. Once He had ascended to heaven and sent upon them the Holy Spirit, the promised Church would be built.

The Church, we know, consists of those redeemed through Christ's blood. This fact Paul cites as a motive when charging the Ephesian elders to be careful in their governing of the church (Acts 20:28). The same Lord who founded the Church also secured it at the cost of His own blood (1 Peter 1:18, 19; Hebrews 9:14).

3. *Empowered and furnished by the Spirit.* After Jesus had ascended to the Father, He sent the Holy Spirit upon the Church. "This Jesus," Peter

explained in his Pentecostal sermon, "... hath shed forth this, which ye now see and hear" (Acts 2:32, 33).

God lives in the midst of the Church in the person of the Holy Spirit. It is difficult if not impossible to imagine a New Testament Church without the manifest presence of the Spirit of God. The use of the word *spirit* in the Bible, even apart from its use in reference to the Third Person of the holy Trinity, demonstrates that the spirit is the principle of life. "The body without the spirit is dead" (James 2:26). What James wrote of the human body is equally true of the body of Christ.

What is the relationship of the Holy Spirit to the Church? Its members are born of the Spirit (John 3:5). It is the Spirit who appoints leaders (Acts 20:28) and gives guidance in missionary activity (13:2). The Spirit distributes His gifts (1 Corinthians 12:11), and "where the Spirit of the Lord is, there is liberty" (2 Corinthians 3:17). It is the Spirit who warns of last-day departures from the faith (1 Timothy 4:1) and who addresses the seven churches of Revelation (2:7, 11, 29; 3:1, 6, 13, 22).

The Church, in summary, is that group of the redeemed who answer God's desire for fellowship by assembling together in Jesus' name and at His call in a society designed by the Father, brought into existence by the Son, and continuously nurtured by the life-giving Spirit. The Church is truly "the church ... in God" (1 Thessalonians 1:1).

How *a* Church Began

The church in Thessalonica is an example of the many individual churches that dot the pages of the New Testament. The story is told in Acts 17:1-5. This church makes a good example, since its origin is described in Acts and since the Holy Spirit has preserved for us two of the letters of Paul (the founder of the church) addressed to this church. In them we glimpse something of the problems of the local church.

Combining the information in Acts and the two Thessalonian epistles with what may be learned from the history of the times, let us see what lessons arise from this early example of the establishment of a particular church.

1. *The city of Thessalonica was itself a seaport town, a commercial center on the chief coastal highway.* It was an important city and one that drew the attention of the apostle because it was yet unreached for Christ. The pattern for missionary evangelism presented in the Book of Acts seems to be to seek out the chief cities of a district, establish a center of belief there, and use this as a base for further operations in the surrounding area.

2. *Preaching that has the Scriptures as its basis and Christ as its contents was the key method in reaching the city.* Paul began with the Jews in their synagogue. He carefully "reasoned with them out of the scriptures" (Acts 17:2). His purpose was clear: he hoped to persuade the Jews that Jesus, the Nazarene carpenter, was the promised Messiah. Today, Gentile Christians say very easily the words Jesus *Christ*. But for a Jew to do this would be either blasphemy or conversion. John wrote his Gospel "that ye might believe that Jesus is the Christ"—that He is the Messiah (*Christ* is the Greek equivalent of the Hebrew *Messiah;* John 20:31).

3. *The results varied.* Some believed, including wellborn Greek gentlemen and exceptional women (Acts 17:4; 1 Thessalonians 1:6). They became exemplary Christians, willing to suffer for their faith (1:6; 2:13, 14) and awaiting the Lord's appearing

(1:10). Others hotly opposed the apostle, eventually resulting in his flight from the city (Acts 17:10).

4. *The church was not without its problems.* They were guilty of theological misunderstanding regarding the Lord's return (1 Thessalonians 4:13). This led some to idleness—they actually quit their jobs and sat down to await the Second Coming—drawing the apostle's rebuke in 2 Thessalonians 3:6-13. Immorality persisted (1 Thessalonians 4:3-7).

We err in thinking the churches of the New Testament had no defects. While the Early Church certainly presents a pattern worthy of imitation in many respects, the fact that the Bible records their defects as well as their achievements should caution us always to follow the Lord of the Church rather than to commit ourselves uncritically to any earthly manifestation of the Church.

The church at Thessalonica was *a* church, a particular manifestation of *the* Church. God is the God of people, not of buildings. He is not solely the God of Baptists, the God of Lutherans, the God of Presbyterians, or the God of Pentecostals. He is the God of individuals who are in a living relationship with His Son, the God of Abraham, Isaac, and Jacob.

Denominations and the Church

We commonly use the word *church* to mean denomination. A brief look at the origin of denominations will complete this survey of the origin of the Church.

1. *The New Testament knows nothing of denominations.* It speaks of "the church." There were differences of opinion, as the division of Paul and Barnabas teaches us (Acts 15:36-41). And differences of theological opinion account for many denominational divisions.

2. *The denomination is not the same as the Church.* The Church consists only of those redeemed by the blood of the Lamb. But it is likely that many denominations enroll members who have had no vital contact with Jesus Christ. The persistent peril of Christendom is to confuse membership in a denomination with membership in the Church. Unfortunately, there are many denominations where this is true.

3. *A survey of church history will reveal how the variety of denominations came about.* What we must see here is that the Father planned, the Son purchased, and the Spirit empowered "one body" (Ephesians 4:4), that this one Body has the Biblical title of "the Church," and that members of denominations may or may not be members of the true church of God.

2

Nature of the Church

What is the nature of the Church the Trinity originated? Rather than outline a technical definition of the Church, we shall do as the Bible does, both with this teaching and with others, we shall illustrate the nature of the Church. The Church, as someone has said of Christian experience, "is better felt than telt."

There are a surprising number of metaphors by which the idea of the Church is presented in the Bible. It is described variously as a city (Hebrews 12:22), a family (Ephesians 3:15), a flock (1 Peter 5:2), a candlestick (Revelation 1:20), God's "husbandry," that is, a garden (1 Corinthians 3:9), the household of God (Ephesians 2:19), and a vineyard. (Matthew 21:41).

In this chapter, we will select for examination four figures not among those mentioned above. These four are more common and more widely known. In all of them you will see obvious characteristics that relate to the true church of God.

About the Word *Church*

The New Testament Greek word for *church*, spelled in English letters, is the word *ekklesia*. Our word *ecclesiastica*, which means "pertaining to the church," is derived from this original Greek word. Although this word has been commonly explained to mean "a called-out group," the use of the word in New Testament times had outgrown any consciousness of such an origin. We usually employ words without taking time to think about their make-up. For example, the last time you used the English word *understand,* did you have any thoughts about "standing under" anyone or anything?

Ekklesia appears 115 times in the New Testament. (Since it was written in Hebrew and not in Greek, the Old Testament does not contain the word at all.) Of these 115 times, *ekklesia* (pronounced EK-klay-SEE-yaw) is translated "church" 112 times and "assembly" three times.

Basically the word means "an assembly, a gathering." It may refer to a political gathering or the meeting of a senate, as it does in Acts 19:39. Or it may describe an assembled mob of people, such as the one whipped up by Demetrius the silversmith—of which it is reported "the more part knew not wherefore they were come together" (v. 32). This usage apears in verses 32 and 41. But apart from these three instances, *ekklesia* is God's gathering, God's assembly, the people of God collectively assembled together.

The Church as a Body

What more descriptive way to picture the people of God than the illustration of the body? Even today we speak of "political bodies" or of "religious bodies" when we describe certain organizations.

The idea of the Church as a Body is one of the apostle Paul's favorite ways of describing the Church. He employed this figure of speech in writing his letters to the churches at Rome (Romans 12:5), Corinth (1 Corinthians 10:17), Ephesus (Ephesians 1:23), and Colossae (Colossians 1:18).

Reread 1 Corinthians 12 to catch the full sweep of the apostle's thought. His subject is the gifts of the Holy Spirit. His purpose is to show that all these are dispersed by the Spirit (count the number of times the word *Spirit* appears in this chapter!) and that, considered together, they make up a proportionate, balanced Body.

Here are four characteristics of the human body that relate to the body of Christ.

1. *Unity.* Did you ever see a body that was not a living unit? Only if it was a lifeless body, a corpse. For a body that is alive is always a unity; each part of it contributing to the total function of the body. Whatever a person does, he does as a unit, as a total individual—body, soul, and spirit. If he sins, all of him sins. If he believes, all of him believes. If he suffers, all of him suffers. Reflecting God's own structure, we were created "in His image." God made men unified individuals.

"For as the body is one . . ." (1 Corinthians 12:12). This is the divine standard for the Church. Differences exist. They are essential. God made the differences. But each difference blends into the whole Body.

The church of Jesus Christ is His body. We are "members in particular." If any local assembly lacks unity, it is falling short of the unity that characterizes the body of Christ. Such unity exists only as long as each member remains in a living relationship with the Head of the Body.

2. *Life.* One obvious feature of the human body is life. Who can define "life"? Yet who does not know when life is absent? Life marks the difference between organizations and organisms. A huge lathe in a steel mill is highly complex and very well organized. But it has no life in itself. If it moves, the power for such motion comes from some external source.

The life of the Church is the life of its Lord. In the Biblical portrayal of the Church as the body of Christ, each individual member is presented as some part—the foot, the ear, the inner organ—other than the Head. The Head of the Church is Jesus Christ (Ephesians 4:15).

We have all seen tragic cases of amputated limbs. But we have never seen anyone live without his head intact. Removal of the head, in fact, was a common form of execution. Yet how many decapitated churches there are! After all, it is eternal life that marks entry into the Church. And the church of Jesus Christ is above all a living organism drawing its life from the Head.

3. *Individuality.* The unity of the Church does not cancel out individuality. Instead, unity in the Church is based on individuality. No institution makes more room for individual differences and abilities than the Church. We are never asked to surrender our identities. We are invited to discover them in the total ministry of the body of Christ.

"To one is given . . . wisdom; to another . . . knowledge . . . ; to another faith . . .; . . . to another prophecy"—and so on through all the gifts. "Are all apostles? are all prophets? are all teachers?" Of course not. "If the whole body were an eye, where were the hearing? If the whole were hearing, where were the smelling?" (1 Corinthians 12:8-10, 17, 29).

How can we determine our position in the body of Christ? By asking the Head what we are. Let each one prayerfully determine to what sphere of service God is calling. It may be a conspicuous ministry like a pastor's. He is the leader, and everyone knows him. He might compare with, say, the hands of the body. Or, God may call a person to an inconspicuous ministry which, although unseen, is vitally important—like unseen glands in the body.

Let those who think their humble ministry of prayer or preparing meals for the visiting evangelist or wrapping bandages for missionary clinics is not important read again God's estimate of their service: "Much more those members of the body, which seem to be more feeble, are necessary: and those members of the body, which we think to be less honorable, upon these we bestow more abundant honor; and our uncomely parts have more abundant comeliness" (vv. 22, 23).

4. *Sympathy*. Have you ever noticed that if you injure part of your body, you seem to hurt all over? Pain can be limited to one part of the body, but the whole individual suffers as a result of the injury. On the other hand, which part of your body gets happy the day before vacation time? Your heart? your emotions? your head? Obviously, the whole body shares in both suffering and the joys of any one part.

It is the same in the body of Christ—at any rate, it should be the same. "And whether one member suffer, all the members suffer with it; or one member be honored, all the members rejoice with it" (v. 26). "But whoso hath this world's good, and seeth his brother have need, and shutteth up his bowels of compassion from him, how dwelleth the love of God in him?" (1 John 3:17).

The Church as a Building

"Ye are God's building." These are the exact words of Scripture found in 1 Corinthians 3:9. And this illustration of the building, a huge structure composed of various construction units and resting on a single foundation, presents another beautiful and instructive illustration of the Church.

What are some characteristics of buildings that teach us about the building of God?

1. *Beauty.* Who has not viewed with awe the magnificent structures produced by the engineers of the modern world? The towering strength and simple beauty of these buildings suggest that there is still something of the image of God left in man. Remember that Jesus said, "I will build my church" (Matthew 16:18).

The beauty of no building exceeds or even equals the glorious beauty of the church of God. The Lord is daily concerned with His church "that he might present it to himself a glorious church, not having spot, or wrinkle, or any such thing; but that it should be holy and without blemish" (Ephesians 5:27).

You can understand, then, why God does everything He can to remove ugliness of any kind from His church.

2. *Structure.* Buildings are not built haphazardly. They sit squarely on a foundation adequate to support the intended structure. Materials of sufficient strength are fitted together with bonds of various kinds: mortar, nails, interlocking fasteners. Rooms are partitioned off according to the intended purpose of the building.

In a similar way the church of Jesus Christ is built. It sits on "the foundation of the apostles and prophets" (2:20). The chief Cornerstone is Jesus Christ himself. Then come the assorted ministries set in the Church (4:11). The bond that cements all together is love—God's love for us, ours for Him, and ours for each other.

Peter speaks of Jesus as a living stone to whom believers come as living stones, and both are welded together into "a spiritual house" (1 Peter 2:4, 5). From this angle, we are the stones and God is the Builder, fitting us into the structure of His church.

But there is another side to this building analogy. In 1 Corinthians 3:10-18 Paul again recognizes Jesus

Christ as the foundation, warning that "other foundation can no man lay than that is laid, which is Jesus Christ" (v. 11). But to this he adds that each man in the Church is himself a builder, and he urges caution about what is built. "If any man's work abide which he hath built thereupon, he shall receive a reward. If any man's work shall be burned, he shall suffer loss: but he himself shall be saved; yet so as by fire" (vv. 14, 15).

So in the Church as God's building, two construction jobs are under way: God is fitting us into His building, and we are building lives on the only true foundation, Jesus Christ.

3. *Utility.* Buildings are built for a purpose. They require effort and expense, both to construct and to maintain. They serve purposes.

God's building also has a purpose. What is the purpose of the Church? Simply said, the purpose of the Church is to evangelize the lost and to educate the saved—evangelism and education. Whatever the Church does that does not ultimately serve these twin purposes is in danger of being burned up as "wood, hay, stubble."

The Church as a Bride

Not only is the Church the body of Christ and God's building, but it is also the bride of Christ. All the tender emotions of love and concern are drawn together in this beautiful analogy. Both Paul and John use this analogy, and many of the parables of Jesus speak of the bride and the bridegroom. Remember too the picture of intimacy presented in the Song of Solomon.

Now let us examine some characteristics of a bride that will open to us further the relationship between Christ and the Church.

1. *Devotion.* This works both ways: Christ loves the Church, and the Church loves Christ. Yet "the church is subject unto Christ" (Ephesians 5:24). Christ is the husband, and the Church is the bride.

The entire section from Ephesians 5:21 to 6:9 contains specific instructions for specific groups—wives, husbands, children, servants, and masters. Paul directs the husbands to love their wives (5:25). Then he supports this counsel by reminding them of Christ's love for the Church. So the apostle makes a very practical application.

2. *Dependence.* "For the husband is the head of the wife, even as Christ is the head of the church" (v. 23). God made the man stronger than the woman. She depends on man and in the marital order of authority is subject to the man, just as man is to Christ and Christ is to God. "O what needless pain we bear," wrote the songwriter, "all because we do not carry everything to God in prayer." May we never forget the blessing of dependence on the Head of the Church!

3. *Expectation.* Her wedding day is perhaps the most memorable day in the life of any wife-to-be. She anticipates it eagerly.

The Church awaits its Lord, just as the Thessalonian believers had turned from idols "to wait for his Son from heaven" (1 Thessalonians 1:10). One truly in love desires the presence of the one loved. And great joy comes through reunion after a long absence. Imagine the bliss of that hour when the Bridegroom returns for His bride who has prepared herself for that day of arrival, even though she did not know the exact time of His return. "And the Spirit and the bride say, Come" (Revelation 22:17). "Surely I come quickly" (v. 20). With these significant sentences the last chapter of the last Book of the Bible closes.

The Church as a Brotherhood

Optimistic "social-gospelers" of a bygone generation attempted to convince everyone that all men are brothers. So far as this is understood to mean that all men are created by God—brothers by creation—this is Biblically accurate. But the Bible points out a difference between brothers by creation and brothers by new creation.

Here is what Jesus has done: through the new birth He has brought all the redeemed together into the community of God, God's gathering, and regardless of wealth, status, or intelligence, they are brothers and sisters in the Lord.

What does brotherhood involve?

1. *Equality.* The right Christian attitude toward our brethren is that any one of us is no better or worse than another. "But why dost thou judge thy brother? or why dost thou set at nought thy brother? for we shall all stand before the judgment seat of Christ" (Romans 14:10).

2. *Responsibility.* You may have the right and the freedom to do something. But you also have a responsibility to your brother. Romans 14 is crucial in Christian community life.

3. *Love.* This "greatest thing in the world" exists wherever people are in living contact with Him who is love (1 John 4:8). "But as touching brotherly love ye need not that I write unto you: for ye yourselves are taught of God to love one another" (1 Thessalonians 4:9). "Love the brotherhood" (1 Peter 2:17).

This, then, is the heritage and the privilege of the Church: the unity of a body, the beauty and stability of a building, the expectancy of a bride, and the fellowship of the brethren (sisters too, we must add!).

3
Scope of the Church

"But who is my brother?" we may ask today, in the spirit of the query a certain lawyer put to Jesus (Luke 10:25, 29). And Jesus' answer parallels His response to the lawyer: our brother (and the lawyer's "neighbor") includes even the one we tend to avoid, the one who is to us as despised as the Samaritan.

The Church is a brotherhood. So it is right to ask, "Who is my brother? my sister?"

Our spiritual siblings do not always wear the same type of clothes we do. Their incomes may not equal ours or they may far exceed ours. Their faces may be a different color. Their language may not be familiar.

Our kinfolk in the body of Christ are, in fact, any and all who believe in Jesus Christ. The one single factor that determines entrance into a blissful eternity spent in the presence of God is purely and simply—or perhaps not so simply—belief. If I believe, I am by Jesus Christ made a brother to everyone else who believes. I have no right to exclude any whom He includes.

For this reason, it is customary to speak of "the invisible Church"—not as though the Church is never seen, for the Church does not exist without being visible. But speaking of an "invisible Church" signifies that throughout the world we have many unknown brothers and sisters who do not speak our language, who have unfamiliar customs and values, and who may not be identified with our particular denomination. This universal body of Christ includes the "whole family in heaven and earth." It is the "household of God" (Ephesians 2:19; 3:15).

Dimensions of the Church

The Church, you recall, is "God's building" (1 Corinthians 3:9). We expect buildings to have dimensions—breadth, height, and depth, unless of course they are merely proposed buildings in the blueprint stage. But the Church is not an idea; it is a reality. The Church has spiritual dimensions.

For its vertical height, its altitude, the Church towers into heaven itself. This edifice in the Spirit stands tall enough to reach God.

For its breadth and length, the Church is worldwide, stretching to every country in which may be found a white heart, without regard to the color of skin covering that sanctified heart. In this respect, the Church is everywhere believers are. For Jesus himself said: "Where two or three are gathered together in my name, there am I in the midst of them" (Matthew 18:20).

For its depth, the Church consists of those who believe, who truly believe, who "believe in depth."

The Breadth of the Church

Let me urge you to make a careful reading of Acts 10, that thrilling record of the Early Church empowered by the Spirit of God. And while reading, go on to verse 18 of the next chapter. As if the Lord wanted no reader to miss this account, He recorded it twice!

Acts 10 reports the experience of a man, a chosen apostle, who had too narrow a view of the wide working of God.

1. *Peter belonged to a group that was extremely*

exclusive, both socially and religiously. Throughout their history, the Jews had been God's chosen people. Even in their birth as a nation with the call of Abraham, God had chosen one particular man out of whom He was going to make a nation (Genesis 12:1, 2). Again and again the prophets reminded the people of Israel that God had specially chosen them, not on the basis of merit or size, but through God's electing grace. Misunderstanding the purpose of this choice by God, the Jews became proud of their exclusiveness and lost the sense of mission for which they had really been chosen.

2. *This group had severe restrictions on associations with outsiders.* The Samaritans were special objects of scorn. Recall the surprise of the woman at the well in Samaria when Jesus asked her for water: "How is it that thou, being a Jew, askest drink of me, which am a woman of Samaria? for the Jews have no dealings with the Samaritans" (John 4:9). When Jesus would show who is the neighbor to a Jew, He gave the Parable of the Good *Samaritan* Luke 10:25-37).

Many readers are familiar with the classic work of Alfred Edersheim titled *The Life and Times of Jesus the Messiah.* The same author wrote a book that is undeservedly lesser known, *Sketches of Jewish Social Life* (London: Religious Tract Society, n.d.). Here is an extended quotation describing the exclusiveness of the Jews:

> Milk drawn from a cow by heathen hands, bread and oil prepared by them, might indeed be sold to strangers, but not used by Israelites. No pious Jew would of course have sat down at the table of a Gentile (Acts 11:3; Galatians 2:12). If a heathen were invited to a Jewish house, he might not be left alone in the room, else every article of food or drink on the table was henceforth to be regarded as unclean. If cooking utensils were bought of

them, they had to be purified by fire or by water; knives to be ground anew, spits to be made red-hot before use, etc. It was not lawful to let either house or field, nor to sell cattle, to a heathen; any article, however distantly connected with heathenism, was to be destroyed. Thus, if a weavingshuttle had been made of wood grown in a grove devoted to idols, every web of cloth made by it was to be destroyed; nay, if such pieces had been mixed with others, to the manufacture of which no possible objection could have been taken, these all became unclean, and had to be destroyed (pp. 27, 28).

With this Jewish exclusiveness in mind, it is easily understood why the first thing Peter mentions in his address to Cornelius and those present is his consciousness of the unusual intimacy he, Peter the Jew, is permitting with Cornelius the Gentile: "Ye know how that it is an unlawful thing for a man that is a Jew to keep company, or come unto one of another nation" (Acts 10:28).

The Heavenly Vision

3. *It took a special vision from God to unfold to Peter God's universal interest in all men.* And the vision itself was repeated three times. In the vision Peter was asked by the voice—either God's or one of His high representatives'—to rise, kill, and eat certain unclean animals that appeared on a sheet suspended from heaven. The command must have had special significance for Peter, since it was noon ("the sixth hour") and since the text expressly says: ". . . and he became very hungry" (Acts 10:9, 10).

Because of his strict training as a Jew, Peter strongly refused to touch these animals which had by the Jewish law been designated unclean. But the voice said to him these great words: "What God hath cleansed, that call not thou common" (v. 15).

Peter puzzled over the meaning of such a vision,

but God had already been at work in circumstances that would shortly disclose the meaning of the strange vision. For some hours earlier God had also spoken to a man—not a Jew—and given him instructions to send for Peter, disclosing not only Peter's identity but also his town of residence and street address. God was working in both hearts at the same time. He worked with Peter to widen his vision of the Church, and He worked—through the very same circumstances—with Cornelius to mature his spiritual experience.

Peter was about to learn the breadth of the Church. He was now ready, after a special vision from God, to recognize God's hand of blessing upon some individuals other than the Jews.

4. *"I should not call any man common or unclean."* This is the lesson Peter learned; the discovery that made him ready to associate with Cornelius. Here is an itemized list of the statements in Acts 10 and 11 that portray Peter's dawning discovery of God's interest in people outside his own group:

a. 10:15: "What God hath cleansed, that call not thou common."

b. 10:28: "God hath showed me that I should not call any man common or unclean."

c. 10:34, 35: "Of a truth I perceive that God is no respecter of persons: but in every nation he that feareth him, and worketh righteousness, is accepted with him."

d. 10:43: "Whosoever believeth in him shall receive remission of sins."

e. 11:17: "Forasmuch then as God gave them the like gift as he did unto us, who believed on the Lord Jesus Christ, what was I, that I could withstand God?"

To certify that He had accepted Cornelius, representative of all Gentiles, into His church, God poured out His Spirit upon the assembled group even while Peter was addressing them. When this happened, the six Jews who had come with Peter were amazed, together with Peter, "that on the Gentiles also was poured out the . . . Holy Ghost" (10:45).

May we learn with Peter that God has "mercy on whom he will have mercy" (Romans 9:18). Let us lift up our eyes and see that "the field is the world" (Matthew 13:38). No people should be repugnant to us. No one is outside the range of God's blessing. In Christ, there are no Samaritans, no Jews, no Gentiles. "For by one Spirit are we all baptized into one body, whether we be Jews or Gentiles, whether we be bond or free" (1 Corinthians 12:13).

5. *The breadth of the Church is therefore all who are accepted by God.* The scope of the Church is indicated in the words *"whosoever* believeth." Some who "believe" may produce in us the same emotion that stunned the seven Jews at Cornelius' house—amazement and astonishment that God would work among such people.

Elsewhere in the New Testament

This was not a problem that Peter alone faced. As a loyal Jew, he had to learn this lesson. But the scope of the Church, its universal reach among all peoples, is treated elsewhere in the New Testament.

Mark preserves an incident in the ministry of Jesus that happened even prior to this incident in the life of Peter:

> And John answered him, saying, Master, we saw one casting out devils in thy name, and he followeth not us; and we forbade him, because he followeth not us. But Jesus said, Forbid him not: for there is no man which shall do a miracle in my name, that can lightly speak evil of me. For he that is not against us is on our part (Mark 9:38-40).

Jesus here trained His disciples to alert themselves to God's work elsewhere.

Through his letters preserved in the New Testament, Paul firmly establishes the universal scope of the true Church. Perhaps no letter does this with greater insistence than Ephesians. Thinking of Jew and Gentile, he writes: "For he is our peace, who hath made both one, and hath broken down the middle wall of partition between us" (2:14). In 3:1-12 he asserts that the melting together of Jew and Gentile in the one true Church is a "mystery," not revealed till unfolded by Paul through the revelation of God to him.

A second quotation from Alfred Edersheim sums up this major point:

> What an almost incredible truth must it have seemed, when the Lord Jesus Christ proclaimed it among Israel as the object of His coming and kingdom, not to make of the Gentiles Jews, but of both alike children of one Heavenly Father; not to rivet upon the heathen the yoke of the law, but to deliver from it Jew and Gentile, or rather to fulfill its demands for all! The most unexpected and unprepared-for revelation, from the Jewish point of view, was that of the breaking down of the middle wall of partition between Jew and Gentile, the taking away of the enmity of the law, and the nailing it to His cross (*Sketches of Jewish Social Life*, pp. 28, 29).

The breadth of the Church, then, is its worldwide sweep, its universal appeal to all men called of God. It is called the "invisible Church" because its total size is known only by God, who alone knows all things. "The Lord knoweth them that are his" (2 Timothy 2:19). There are doubtless many whom we assume to be members of the Church who really are not. And also there may be many within the body of Christ whom we do not suspect.

One of the greatest surprises of heaven will be

who is there! The next greatest surprise will be who is not there! "Many will say to me in that day, Lord, Lord, have we not prophesied in thy name? and in thy name have cast out devils? and in thy name done many wonderful works? And then will I profess unto them, I never knew you: depart from me, ye that work iniquity" (Matthew 7:22, 23).

The Church in Depth

The depth of the Church is the dimension of *belief*. There are other ways to describe what brings about eternal life: the new birth, regeneration, justification by faith, and so on. But these all seem to be contained or implied in the single concept of belief.

We have from John's Gospel the word of Jesus: "He that believeth on him is not condemned: but he that believeth not is condemned already" (John 3:18). And notice that while both belief and baptism are prescribed for salvation in Mark 16:16, when the verse goes on to spell out the conditions for damnation it omits baptism and specifies unbelief as the sole basis for damnation.

So in the notion of belief we wrap up all that makes the eternal difference between the saved and the lost; between those in the Church and those out of it. It is quite important, therefore, that we understand what the Bible means by belief.

What is belief? Three ideas (based on the Hebrew and Greek words translated "belief") explain the Biblical idea of belief.

1. *Persuasion.* One important element of belief is persuasion that a thing is true. One cannot be expected to throw himself upon a belief that he is not mentally convinced is true. There is, therefore, a

mental or intellectual side to belief. We must love God with all our minds (Luke 10:27).

Some examples from the Bible will make this clear. The chief priests and the elders did not know how to respond to Jesus' question about the origin of John's baptism. Part of their dilemma was that the people were *"persuaded* that John was a prophet" (20:6). When Gamaliel gave sound counsel to the assembled Jewish council, "to him they *agreed*" (Acts 5:40). Tragically, King Agrippa said, "Almost thou *persuadest* me to be a Christian" (26:28). When Paul preached to the Thessalonians, "some of them *believed*" (17:4). (Compare also 18:4; 19:8, 9.)

In all these instances, the Greek word translated by the italicized words above has as its basic meaning "to be convinced mentally that a thing is true."

2. *Commitment.* Mental agreement is necessary, but it is not sufficient. One must also entrust himself entirely to someone or something; in the case of Christian belief, to God through Christ. A second factor in Biblical belief is total commitment of oneself—body, soul, spirit, mind, emotions, abilities (and inabilities!), and resources.

To Paul the gospel was "committed" (Galatians 2:7). Though men apparently "believed" in Jesus because of the miracles He did, "Jesus did not commit himself unto them, because he knew all men." Though it is not obvious in English, the words *believed* and *commit* in this passage found in John 2:23, 24 are the same in Greek. This is John's word—he uses it 100 times in his Gospel. Paul preached commitment: "With the heart man believeth unto righteousness" (Romans 10:10).

3. *Steadfastness.* Here is the Biblical pattern for belief: first you are persuaded that something is true, then you commit yourself to it, and, finally, you must remain steadfast in that commitment.

The little word *amen* originated in a Hebrew word that really means "to be firm." Saying, "Amen," then, means, "Let this that has been said be firmly established." When Genesis reports of Abraham, "And he believed in the Lord" (15:6), it uses this basic word. To believe is to remain steadfast in the commitment one has made.

Here then is the Church: in height, reaching to God himself; in breadth, sweeping around the world wherever God is at work; in depth, residing in every heart mentally agreed to the message of the gospel, totally committed to Christ, and continuously abiding in confident steadfastness.

4

Message of the Church

The Church is essentially evangelistic: it has an evangel, a message of glad tidings. There are many ways and words useful in describing this message, for it is a message of unbelievable breadth. One word, perhaps, best describes what the Church has to say. That word is *wholeness*.

God created man whole. But since the Fall, he and his world have been broken into an endless number of fragments. Broken minds fill our mental institutions. Broken bodies fill our hospitals. Broken marriages are listed matter-of-factly in our newspapers. Broken international relations perpetuate the tensions of the Cold War. Even the Christian Church itself, with its many denominational divisions, reveals the splintering effect of the Fall.

God's goal in the world is completeness, soundness, health, and perfection. Through Christ wholeness is now possible—wholeness in body, soul, and spirit; wholeness in history, society, and the Church.

The message of the Church is the message of its Lord. To the impotent man at the pool of Bethesda He said, "Wilt thou be made whole?" The pitiable response of the sick man typifies the sigh of lost man in today's fragmented world: "Sir, I have no man" (John 5:6, 7). It is the privilege of the Church to become that man, to bring about wholeness and healing to an impotent world.

Wholeness in Soul—Salvation

Wholeness is the message the Church offers to the world. The gospel is only a "full" gospel if it is concerned with the whole nature of man.

The Pentecostal movement has customarily summarized its leading doctrinal emphases in four well-known points: salvation, divine healing, the baptism in the Holy Spirit, and the Second Coming. Each of these four designates an area in which brokenness has occurred and in which wholeness is vitally needed.

What exactly is wholeness? More familiar is the word *whole*. The state or condition of being whole is called wholeness. Here is a definition of *whole* taken from an unabridged dictionary: "being uninjured or without signs of injury; of a wound, healed: more widely, sound and healthy or restored to soundness and health, as of body, mind, or soul; in perfect condition physically and mentally; not broken or defective; undamaged, intact; containing all its constituent parts." God gave His Son to secure precisely this state in man.

The word *whole* has some surprising relatives in the English language. It comes from the very same root word as the word *holy*. In fact, it is true to say that holiness is wholeness. *Heal* and *health* both describe wholeness, usually (though not exclusively) physical. *Hallow* (as in the Lord's Prayer, "Hallowed be thy name") means to reckon holy, whole, entire, the name of God. *Holiday* was originally a holy day. A *halibut* got its name from a "holy fish"—holy because it was to be eaten when other meats were forbidden by some parts of the Early Church. *Halloween,* curiously, is a corruption of "hallowed evening," the evening before the day celebrated as All Saints Day.

Biblical words for wholeness emphasize health, prosperity, and deliverance, in addition to separation from what is unwhole and consecration to Him who is perfect in wholeness.

Salvation is the personal reception of wholeness in soul. By being "saved" we mean that we have placed ourselves in the stream of God's healing grace and mercy. We invite Him to make us whole in soul. We become healed of man's greatest and most disastrous disease—sin. In a moment, by one touch of the Healer's hand, we become whole. We become, through Christ, righteous in God's eyes. This does not mean that immediately every problem is solved. But it does mean that we are declared whole and that we are now attended by the divine Physician of souls—Jesus Christ.

Crisis or Process?

Are we saved in a crisis or through a process? Both. Most Christians will testify that their conversion was the climax of a process of God's tender dealing with their souls. Those saved as children may not recall any such crisis; it lies buried in their memories. The important fact is not the way it happened, but whether or not it actually did happen.

Salvation is the present possession of spiritual soundness. Whether or not one has come to this present state by crisis or by process, the issue is: has he reached wholeness in salvation? This is why we must never rest on past experience but must always have an up-to-date experience with the Lord. One Biblical word to describe this experience is *abiding,* especially characteristic of John 15 and the epistle of 1 John.

Holiness should be understood as wholeness. It is a word given to describe the degree to which we have personally appropriated the provisions of God for wholeness in our own lives. First Thessalonians 5:23 is Paul's prayer, his wish, for the believers to whom he writes. He desires that every facet of their being—body, soul, and spirit—be set apart to God and be found without blame at the coming of Jesus.

Being wholly set apart to God may mean different things to different people, but "let every man be fully persuaded in his own mind" (Romans 14:5). There is no inward difference between two persons who are wholly committed to God. They both seek to please and serve Him. But background and training play important roles in how this inward dedication is expressed outwardly.

One should be careful in evaluating the dedication of another solely by appearance. Indeed, we are not called to be judges of another man's servant (v. 4). Yet, since God's goal is wholeness, the holiness of the soul will show itself in the holiness of the body. Unfortunately, it does not work the other way around. One is not spiritually holy just because he looks that way. Remember 1 Samuel 16:7: "Man looketh on the outward appearance, but the LORD looketh on the heart."

Wholeness in Body—Divine Healing

You are an individual. Everyone is an individual. No two of us are exactly alike. Lengthy theological debates have been staged regarding the nature of man. Is the human person three parts—body, soul, and spirit? Or is he two parts—material and invisible? This controversy, as most, is needless. Whether one recognizes two or three divisions in the nature of man, neither of these should obscure the fact that man is primarily a unit, an individual.

"The body without the spirit is dead" (James

2:26), and who sees his spirit? "A spirit hath not flesh and bones" (Luke 24:39). The people you know are people with flesh, bones, blood, body, soul, spirit, mind, and strength—all together in one living whole.

Sometimes, by a figure of speech, the whole individual is designated by a part. In 1 Peter 3:20, eight "souls" were in the ark, while in 1:24, all "flesh" is like grass. In both instances, it is clear that people are being discussed. Compare this with the naval officer's command, "All hands on deck!"

Jesus died for people, not for parts of people. When the Bible and those who believe it refer to the "salvation of the soul," they mean more than that the invisible soul of man may be saved. Since the soul of man is the enduring part of his nature, it alone is mentioned in the phrase "salvation of the soul." Not only is the soul saved; but participating in that "so great salvation" are also the mind, the spirit, the strength, and even the body—indeed the whole nature of man.

So the body too may share in the message of wholeness offered by the Church. There is a gospel for the body as there is for the soul. The physical decay, deformity, disease, and death we see on every hand in today's world do not express the deepest desires of the Father. It is God's will that everyone be physically whole, just as it is His desire that none perish spiritually.

Many miracles in the Gospels show physical and spiritual wholeness linked together. An example is the story of the woman healed of an issue of blood (Mark 5:25-34). After she had touched Him, Jesus said to the persistent woman, "Go in peace." This expression is a good Old Testament way of expressing spiritual soundness. Then He said also—this time of her healed body—"Be whole of thy plague."

Similarly, Isaiah 53:5 ties together spiritual wholeness ("He was wounded for our transgressions") with physical wholeness ("and with his stripes we are healed").

But if it is truly God's will that all be physically whole, why are some not healed in answer to prayer? We do not know all the answers. But we do know some. We know unconfessed sin hinders prayer (Psalm 66:18). We know persistence is essential (Luke 18:1). We know God has His own purposes in delaying the answer (v. 7).

Physical wholeness appears in two stages. The first is every instance of a supernatural miracle of healing. The second is the perfection of the body at the resurrection. It is a great confidence to know that Christian believers who haven't been healed will have new bodies at the resurrection.

But God also heals in this life, now. Like Jesus' disciples, we are often tempted to think that a sick Christian is a sinning Christian. To us, as to His disciples, Jesus speaks: "Neither hath this man sinned, nor his parents: but that the works of God should be made manifest in him" (John 9:3).

To give a divine demonstration of His ultimate design, God heals people today. The reasons some are healed and others are not are among "the secret things" that "belong unto the LORD our God" (Deuteronomy 29:29). Whenever God does heal, He bursts through from eternity into time and displays His limitless power and loving desire for the wholeness of His people. Who knows but that a person's affliction exists "that the works of God should be made manifest in him" (John 9:3)?

Wholeness in Spirit—The Baptism in the Holy Spirit

Not only does the Church offer a message of

wholeness in soul and in body, but it also offers wholeness in spirit. The spirit of man is the inner invisible part of him that seems to be the very principle of life itself. In fact, both in Hebrew and in Greek the words for spirit are also translated breath and wind.

But we are not complete in spirit until our spirits are filled with God's Spirit. The Bible speaks of the experience by which this complete fullness is brought as the baptizing work of the Holy Spirit. When John the Baptist sought a single sentence to contrast his own ministry with the Lord's, he did it by showing how much greater it would be to baptize in the Holy Spirit than to baptize merely in water (Mark 1:8). In His final interview with His disciples before ascending to heaven, Jesus instructed them to return to Jerusalem promising, "Ye shall be baptized with the Holy Ghost not many days hence" (Acts 1:5).

The baptism in the Holy Spirit is, therefore, an experience that normally (but not necessarily) takes place some time after one has become a Christian. It brings the believer into an unprecedented place of spiritual power and potential. The Samaritan converts (through the evangelistic ministry of Philip, the anointed deacon) had believed and been baptized in water. But the Holy Spirit was yet to fall on them (8:12-17).

The Ephesian Pentecost reveals clearly the wholeness in spirit secured through the arrival of the Holy Spirit personally and inwardly. Finding they knew only the baptism of John, Paul was concerned that the brethren be complete in spirit. So he asked, "Have ye received the Holy Ghost since ye believed?" (19:2). This verse may also be translated, "Did ye receive the Holy Ghost when ye believed?" The important thing is not when it happened, but whether or not it had ever happened. Either translation reveals that it is God's will that the Christian's experience be marked by the wholeness in spirit that comes through directly encountering the Holy Spirit of God.

Dividing Christian experience into units or "definite works" may be useful for analysis and description. But we are too often guilty of dividing asunder what God has joined together. We must see from this passage that the total wholeness offered by God to man as a part of redemption includes what has been called the baptism in the Holy Spirit. And the word *baptism* itself, of course, suggests a complete, entire, and overwhelming immersion in the Holy Spirit of God.

Wholeness in History—The Second Coming

True Christians always have been conscious of the certainty of the Lord's second coming. Popular Bible study, through the study of dispensations and prophecy, has combined with the rapid change of world events to excite wide interest in the coming of the Lord.

Yet a danger has been to become overconcerned with the sequence of events of the last times, at the expense of their true significance. It is unwise to become so interested in the time of the Lord's coming that we become blind to the Person who is coming.

We usually think of history in terms of kings and battles, colonies and inventions, discoveries and explorations. But history is also another name for time, as opposed to eternity. The Bible teaches a God-centered view of time—or of history. And it discloses that all time leans forward toward the end of time itself. There is coming a day when history will be complete, when once again time will be full. That season will begin with the blessed hope of the Christian—the return of the Lord from heaven. When He comes, He will bring about the completion of time. Here are a few of the things that will happen:

1. *Knowledge will become perfect.* Our minds now suffer the effects of the Fall. When the Lord comes, our minds will become fully whole. "Then shall I know even as also I am known" (1 Corinthians 13:12).

2. *Physical bodies will become perfect.* All shall receive new bodies "fashioned like unto his glorious body" (Philippians 3:21). What prayers for physical healing are unanswered here on earth will certainly be answered there on that great day.

3. *Justice will arrive.* The wicked will be punished. Christians who lived on earth and saw the wicked prosper will see the wicked brought to their appropriate end. All wrongs will be made right.

4. *The redeemed will be blessed.* With new bodies free from disease and limitation, with full knowledge, and with unimpaired fellowship with God, the great Church, the body of Christ, will enjoy her God forever.

5

The Lord's Supper

In proclaiming its needed message of wholeness, the Church, the body of Christ and the building of God, carries out an ongoing program of preaching, teaching, and healing—just as its Head did. In addition to these activities, the Church administers the ordinances instituted by Jesus, the Lord's Supper and baptism in water.

These two ordinances are among the "means of grace," the ways by which spiritual life is secured and maintained. Among the "means of grace" are such activities as attending public worship, prayer—public and private, reading the Bible as God's Word, and the preaching of the Word.

There is little difference between the meanings of the word *ordinance* and the word *sacrament*. The Roman Catholic Church recognizes seven rites which it calls "sacraments." Protestants limit these to the two specifically commanded by Christ. Because of the Roman Catholic use of the term *sacrament*, some Protestants prefer the term *ordinance*. Either term is in itself acceptable.

Anticipated

The Lord's Supper was the Christian replacement for the Passover Feast of the Jews. The New Testament itself asserts: "For even Christ our passover is sacrificed for us" (1 Corinthians 5:7).

For over 400 years, the Children of Israel had been in bondage and under servitude in Egypt. The time had come for their deliverance. God thought this so significant an event that He said Israel would redate their calendar from the miraculous day of deliverance (Exodus 12:2).

But to secure deliverance, God's way must be followed. God always has a way out, if man will but follow it, instead of laboring under his own methods. And God's way involved blood (vv. 7, 22, 23). Each family would select an unblemished lamb and strike its blood upon the doorpost. At a given hour, the Lord would go through the land and take the life of the oldest child in every household in Egypt—except those whose doors were spotted with the protecting blood (vv. 12, 13). The body of the slain lamb was to be roasted and eaten in readiness for departure (vv. 8, 11).

All this actually happened (vv. 50, 51). As a result, the Children of Israel would perpetually celebrate the great deliverance by observing ever after the Passover Feast annually (vv. 24, 25). When the children would ask what the celebration meant, it would provide an opportunity to explain what a great thing God had done for Israel (vv. 26, 27).

The Passover prefigured God's deliverance of all who believe from bondage in sin. Such a deliverance involves applying, to the door of one's heart, the precious blood of the unblemished Lamb—Jesus Christ (1 Peter 1:19). When this happens, new life begins—the calendar is revised (John 3:3; 2 Corinthians 5:17). When we as believing individuals come out of sin by God's mighty grace, it is our personal "exodus."

Just as Israel celebrated the deliverance wrought

for them by God, so the Christian Church at the institution of Jesus Christ periodically observes with joy the release from the bondage of sin by sharing in the Lord's Supper. It is in this sense that the Passover Feast of the Old Testament constitutes an anticipation of the Lord's Supper in the New Testament.

Instituted

The Jews were still observing the practice of celebrating the Passover at the time of Jesus. It is generally believed that Jesus himself was crucified on the very day during the Passover feast when the lamb was slain. It was the last evening of Jesus' life in His earthly body; it was not yet in its glorified state. The next day He would be crucified. That evening—already "the next day" by the Jewish manner of reckoning a day as beginning with sunset of the preceding day—was the evening of the Passover meal.

It was during the very observance of the Passover meal of the Jews, which Jesus himself as a Jew observed, that the events took place which we call "the Last Supper." At this last supper with His disciples, during the Passover meal, Jesus instituted the Lord's Supper.

Picture the deep emotion of that night. Jesus knows He will be crucified the next day. One of His disciples will betray Him when the supper is over and will take his own life. The Jewish nation He loves, which will slay the Passover lamb, will also in a few hours slay the Lamb of God. "The Lord Jesus, the same night in which he was betrayed, took bread" (1 Corinthians 11:23). While His own life is about to be taken, He founds an ordinance symbolizing that this life will forever be shared by those who will eat the Bread of Life.

But all is not gloom. With the institution of the Lord's Supper, Jesus promises that a day will come when He will eat again with them in the kingdom of God. With this simple act, and with the command, "This do in remembrance of me" (Luke 22:19), Jesus institutes the Lord's Supper.

Practiced

Records of the Early Church show us several things about the continuation of the Lord's Supper. The passage in Acts 2:42, 46, and 47 consists of Luke's summary of the activities of the early Christians. He includes, as one of their regular devotional practices, the "breaking of bread." This is another term for the Lord's Supper. (Compare 1 Corinthians 10:21, where it is also called "the Lord's table.")

The passage about Paul's lengthy sermon, during which Eutychus fell out of the window, suggests by its language that meeting together for the breaking of bread was the specific purpose of Christian assembly. "The disciples came together to break bread" (Acts 20:7).

In the Book of Acts, then, we learn that the ordinance that Jesus had founded had been established by His followers as (apparently) a weekly observance. Jesus himself had specified no frequency. He merely said: "This do ye, as oft as ye drink it, in remembrance of me" (1 Corinthians 11:25). We see the Lord's Supper had become even then a regular part of their religious services.

Interpreted

So the Lord's Supper was anticipated in the Passover, instituted by the Lord, and practiced by the apostles. What does the Lord's Supper mean? Eight factors are important in interpreting the Lord's Supper.

1. *Fellowship.* "As they were eating..." (Matthew 26:26). You know the joys of dining with friends and family. The Lord's Supper was instituted in just such an atmosphere. This Lord's Supper, however, was charged with all the urgency and deep feeling that must have filled the heart of the Son of God who was eating with the sons of men. Jesus, in giving himself, gave the Bread of Life. "They continued ... in the apostles' doctrine and fellowship" (Acts 2:42). Around the table of the Lord there is fellowship—with Him and with His.

2. *Obedience.* "This do ye ..." (1 Corinthians 11:25). Observance of the Lord's Supper is not optional with each individual believer; it is the specific command of the Lord himself. The same was true of the Passover celebration. God commanded Israel to observe it regularly throughout their days. Let those who refuse to accept the Communion cup give heed to this feature of the Supper. It is only misunderstanding or continued and unrepented sin that could possibly deter one from willingly fulfilling this command of the Lord.

3. *Memory.* "... in remembrance of me" (Luke 22:19). The Passover looked back on God's great deliverance of the Children of Israel through the Red Sea. By it they recognized and recalled thankfully their exodus. In the same way, the Lord's Supper looks backwards. Sitting at the table of the Lord, one who believes lifts his eyes to Calvary where He sees suspended for him the true Lamb of God, whose shed blood has been applied to his own heart. At the Lord's table, we remember the Lord whose table it is. He is sitting there.

4. *Redemption.* "My blood, which is shed for you"

(v. 20). There is more than mere memory associated with the Lord's Supper. This meal establishes in a peculiar way the "new testament," which displaced the old covenant. There is a redemptive theme in the Lord's Supper: "This is my blood of the new testament, which is shed for many for the remission of sins" (Matthew 26:28); ". . . which is shed for you" (Luke 22:20). "This is my body which is given for you" (v. 19). We are not expected to believe that the elements of the Lord's Supper, the bread and the wine, actually in themselves contain some sort of magical regenerating power. In the Lord's Supper, the redeemed recall their redemption.

5. *Union.* "I am the bread of life" (John 6:35). The illuminating comment of W. H. Griffith Thomas on John 6 is in itself enough to clarify this point:

> We are taught that it is not sufficient merely to trust Christ, but there must be something in the spirit which corresponds to eating in the body, a reception of Him in our inmost soul until His will and nature become a part of ours, and, like food, strengthen all our faculties. There is nothing in our nature that so closely corresponds to this assimilation of Christ and our union with Him as eating and drinking, and it is, therefore, used here *(Principles of Theology* [London: Church Book Room, 1965], p. 390).

6. *Judgment.* "Let a man examine himself" (1 Corinthians 11:28). There are two attitudes to avoid in regard to the Lord's Supper: (1) an overdone feeling of unworthiness leading to abhorrence or refusal, and (2) a lighthearted unconcern bordering on irreverence. None of us has any worthiness outside of Christ. If no unconfessed sin is presented to the mind or conscience by the Holy Spirit, let a man partake. On this judgment, note well 1 Peter 4:17.

7. *Proclamation.* "Ye do show the Lord's death

..." (1 Corinthians 11:26). The word "show" is the same one translated elsewhere "preach" and "declare." Celebrating the Lord's Supper is a sort of visualized drama of the death of the Lord. Here, as elsewhere, we preach by our acts.

8. *Expectation.* "... till he come" (v. 26). The Lord's Supper not only looks backward in memory and commemoration, but it anxiously peers into the future when, at a date known only to the Father, the Lord will again dine with them that are His!

Consummated

In the future, we will no longer celebrate the Lord's Supper as we do here on earth. The deep, inner desires for spiritual intimacy with God will be fulfilled beyond the power of human language to describe. Instead of the Lord's Supper as an ordinance, we will be seated at the great Marriage Supper of the Lamb. (See Revelation 7:16, 17; 19:9.) Instead of sitting at the table of the Lord with our few fellow church members, we will sit down with the whole church of God! Even Abraham, Isaac, and Jacob will be there, as well as beloved kinsmen who preceded us to the presence of the Lord.

All this is a part of what in the previous chapter was called "wholeness in history." It is almost beyond our understanding to grasp the immensity of the filling-up of all things that will be accomplished at and with the coming of the Lord.

Till then, we sit "with gladness and singleness of heart" (Acts 2:46) at the table of the Lord and thankfully "show the Lord's death till he come"!

6
Water Baptism

The second ordinance instituted by Jesus Christ is water baptism. These two, water baptism and the Lord's Supper, are the two ordinances of the Church accepted and practiced by Protestants.

Some believe baptism in itself saves. This is a wrong teaching and can lead to severe spiritual damage. By removing attention from the attitudes of the heart and focusing on external rites, such an attitude leaves behind true spiritual experience. The water, the wine, and the bread ever remain what they are chemically. They do not change mysteriously nor do they produce magical spiritual effects. They mean little when not accompanied by the right attitudes of faith, repentance, and confidence in the finished work of Christ.

Anticipated

While the Lord's Supper is related to the continuation of the Christian life, water baptism is related to the origination of that life. This is why the Lord's Supper is taken at regular intervals, while baptism in water is experienced once near the beginning of Christian experience.

The word translated *baptize* in the New Testament means to dip, to immerse, to plunge, to drench, to sink, to overwhelm. Examples from Greek literature could be cited to demonstrate this meaning. The word is used, for example, to describe a ship sinking in the sea. It is used to describe a man who took too deep a financial plunge and as a result was overwhelmed by debt. It is used to indicate martyrdom in which one becomes overwhelmed with death. But the ordinary religious usage of the word signifies immersion in water as a sign of a spiritual experience wrought in the heart.

There are three different and unrelated incidents in the Old Testament that prefigure water baptism. We know they were meant to anticipate water baptism because in the New Testament each one is brought in where water baptism is being discussed.

1. *The Flood* (1 Peter 3:18-21). In this passage the apostle Peter is describing an incident in the ministry of Jesus in which He "preached unto the spirits in prison." Commentators are not agreed as to the meaning of this difficult passage, but that does not hinder our purpose. We are told that eight souls or persons, were rescued by the ark which floated on the water. So Peter says, "Eight souls were saved by water" (v. 20). He does not mean that the water itself saved them, but that their protection in the ark floating on top of the water effected their deliverance from the wide destruction worked by the Flood.

The Flood with its abundance of water suggested water baptism to Peter. He draws a parallel: just as the water was instrumental in delivering the family of Noah, so baptism in water marks the deliverance of Christians from sin. "Baptism doth also now save us" (v. 21). Baptismal water by itself does not save, any more than flood waters do. But in both there may be discerned some relationship between deliverance and water. The Flood, therefore, anticipated water baptism by tying together deliverance and water.

2. *The Exodus* (1 Corinthians 10:1, 2). In this remarkable passage Paul looks back to the crossing of the Red Sea by the Children of Israel and calls that event a baptism unto Moses. Remember how the sea divided and the Children of Israel passed over on dry ground (Exodus 14:22). As if he had both ordinances in mind, Paul goes on to say that the same Children of Israel ate and drank Christ—words that sound much like the Lord's Supper (vv. 3, 4).

Crossing the Red Sea marked the deliverance of Israel from the land of Egypt. Christian baptism marks the release of the individual believer from the bondage of personal sin. Here again water is related to deliverance.

3. *Circumcision* (Colossians 2:11, 12). In quite a different sense from the Flood and the Exodus, circumcision anticipates water baptism. Genesis 17:9-14 gives the account of the appointed seal of the covenant God made with Abraham. Every male was to be circumcised on the 8th day of his life. This was the covenant sign; the token of full membership in the Jewish race.

Circumcision prefigures water baptism in that both are external rites attesting God's covenant. The one relates to the old covenant, and the other concerns the new covenant. Each is a purely physical action, but each has a deeper spiritual significance.

In summary, the Flood and the Exodus anticipate water baptism by virtue of their relationship to water and to previous spiritual deliverance. Circumcision anticipates water baptism by virtue of its covenant-sealing character.

Instituted

Jesus instituted the Christian ordinance of water baptism. But before Him, His cousin, John the Baptist, began preaching a baptism of repentance. Each, therefore, had a share in the institution of baptism.

1. *By John the Baptist.* The mission of John the Baptist was to announce the arrival of the hoped-for Messiah. This Messiah, Jesus Christ, was not the political deliverer the Jews erroneously expected. He would not instigate a rebellion and throw off the embarrassing shackles of Rome, thereby restoring the independence and glory of Israel. For the Messiah was a spiritual deliverer. "He shall save his people from their sins"—this was the promise of the angel (Matthew 1:21).

To be ready for the Messiah would, therefore, demand spiritual preparation. This goal John secured with a baptism of repentance. From surrounding areas many came and confessed their sins, receiving John's baptism. John created no small stir, and the Pharisees and their kind refused that baptism (Luke 7:30). It became necessary for the Jewish authorities to send messengers to John to question him as to his identity (John 1:19).

While John offered a baptism in water—"much water" (3:23)—he was careful to serve only as a forerunner. He repeatedly said, in effect, "True, I am baptizing in water. But look! Soon One will come who will baptize not only in water, but in the Holy Ghost" (Matthew 3:11). John was very conscious of the secondary importance of being immersed in water as compared to being immersed in the Spirit. (Incidentally, no form of the word *baptism* is used in the Old Testament; this is a New Testament concept.)

2. *By Jesus.* By what He said and by what He did, Jesus instituted water baptism. Though John was overcome with a sense of unworthiness, Jesus insisted that for Him to receive John's baptism was the right thing to do (vv. 13-16). His example is binding

on those who follow Him: "He that saith he abideth in him ought himself also so to walk, even as he walked" (1 John 2:6).

In the Great Commission Jesus' chief command was to produce disciples among the nations. To do this His servants were to follow a program of (1) *going* to the nations, wherever they are; (2) *baptizing* converts; and (3) *teaching* such baptized disciples to observe Jesus' teachings. With His command and His example, Jesus instituted the ordinance of water baptism.

Practiced

Examining the pattern set by the Early Church in the Book of Acts yields an awareness of the importance attached to water baptism. Here are some features.

1. *Water baptism was widely experienced and reported.* Among the groups and persons whose water baptisms are recorded are the following: 3,000 on the Day of Pentecost (2:41); Simon (8:13); the Ethiopian eunuch (8:38); Paul (9:18); Cornelius (10:48); Lydia (16:15); the Philippian jailer and his household (16:33); the Corinthians (18:8); and the Ephesians (19:5).

2. *Water baptism regularly followed repentance and belief.* Philip's condition spelled out in answer to the eunuch's request for baptism was simply: "If thou believest with all thine heart, thou mayest" (8:37).

3. *There is no clear example of the baptism of infants.* Some see in Acts 16:33—"he and all his"— an implication that children were included when the jailer was baptized. But there is neither clear command nor undisputed example to baptize infants.

Interpreted

1. *The fundamental meaning of baptism is immersion into the nature of God.* This experience is first spiritual and takes place at conversion. It is next outward and physical, taking place when a minister momentarily submerges a believer under water. The physical portrays a spiritual event.

2. *Water baptism is not the same as conversion nor is it identical with the baptism in the Holy Spirit.* There are, in fact, four baptisms through which a Christian may pass. The accompanying chart will clarify these four actual and possible baptisms. The subject of the baptism is the one who experiences it. The agent is the one who administers it. The medium is that into which the subject is plunged:

Chart of Christian Baptisms

Type	Reference	Subject	Agent	Medium
Salvation	1 Cor. 12:13	Sinner	Holy Spirit	Body of Christ
Water Baptism	Matt. 28:19; Acts 8:38	Believer	Minister	Water
Baptism in the Holy Spirit	Matt. 3:11; Acts 2:33	Believer	Christ	Holy Spirit
Baptism in Suffering	Luke 12:50; Phil. 1:29	Christ and His followers	God	Severe trials, possibly death

3. *The use of water in this ordinance suggests the cleansing action of regeneration on the soul.* Some passages almost sound as though baptism itself saves (see Acts 2:38; 22:16; Mark 16:16; Titus 3:5). We know from the example of the thief on the cross that baptism in water is not a saving agent because he had no opportunity in life to be baptized (Luke 23:39-43).

4. *Water baptism as an ordinance of Christ signifies entrance into the visible Church, just as con-*

version secures entrance into the invisible Church. By water baptism we outwardly identify ourselves with Christ and with the local assembly. Consistency would demand water baptism before acceptance on the church membership rolls. This is the practice on many mission fields.

5. *Water baptism reenacts all Christ has done for us.* By going under the water we imitate Christ's death and burial. Coming out parallels His resurrection. Going up from the baptismal water anticipates the "newness of life." How many Christians have had their sins forgiven by "dying with Christ," yet—figuratively speaking—still lie sleeping in the tomb? Jesus invites all to walk with Him in brand-new resurrection life.

Consummated

Each of the Christian baptisms plunges the believer into God, spiritually speaking. At no time will our immersion into the presence of God be so complete as when God becomes "all in all": "And when all things shall be subdued unto him, then shall the Son also himself be subject unto him that put all things under him, that God may be all in all" (1 Corinthians 15:28). This is part of the hope of the redeemed. It is expressed in wonderful words in Revelation 21:23, 24:

> And the city had no need of the sun, neither of the moon, to shine in it: for the glory of God did lighten it, and the Lamb is the light thereof. And the nations of them which are saved shall walk in the light of it: and the kings of the earth do bring their glory and honor into it.

While this is the hope of the redeemed, what an awful plight the unredeemed face. For we also read in this same Book of Revelation about a final baptism of the lost. Their end is to be baptized in the lake of fire. Those who spurn the grace of God here, who will not accept the Christian baptisms, must in that day endure a baptism of fire.

7

Organization of the Church

The Church, as we have seen, is the body of Christ. Of this Body, He is the Head. This means all direction for the Body, all its thinking, comes from the Head. And it also means the life of the Church is the same as that of its Lord.

Now consider the organization of the Church. It is not correct to say the Early Church was not organized. True, it was not set up in the highly refined structure that developed in subsequent centuries. But already on the pages of the New Testament administrative steps were taken and offices developed as the need for them arose.

We shall see how the organization of the Church did not reduce the life of the Church but instead stimulated it. Organization that allows the Church to live and breathe as a vital organism is desirable and even necessary.

Some Christian groups have a narrow concept of the ministry. But the Reformation reminds us that we are all priests before God. We will examine here the offices of ministry set by God in the Church and consider as well the contribution to the ministry of the Church and its organization made by members of the Body not specifically serving as pastors.

The standards expected of ministers in their daily Christian living and genuine Christian experience are not different from those expected of the lay membership of the churches. Holiness is not the special property of the clergy but the will of God for every believer.

The Management of the Church

The Church is the body of Christ, the building of God, and the temple of the Holy Spirit. That is an expanded way of saying the Church is owned and operated by the threefold holy Trinity. When he itemized the gifts of the Spirit, Paul referred to each member of the Trinity: "... the same Spirit" (1 Corinthians 12:4); "... the same Lord" (v. 5); "... the same God" (v. 6).

To see how the Church is managed, we will first consider some general principles that appear in God's control of the Church. Then we will dip into the records of the Early Church and gaze at the activities that took place there.

Some Guiding Principles

1. *The supreme Head of the Church is Jesus Christ.* It is His church, His body; He "built" it. Considering Christ as its Head, the Church is, in terms of political theory, an absolute monarchy ruled exclusively by one person, Christ.

What does the Head do?

a. He provides life. No one lives without his head. The Church cannot survive without living attachment to its Head.

b. He makes plans. As the builder of the Church, the Lord himself lays the strategy for adding to His body such as should be saved. It is up to the human heads, His understudies, to secure their orders from the Head.

c. He provides unity for all the members of the Body. We have 2 ears, 2 hands, 2 feet, 10 toes, 10 fingers, hundreds of bones, and billions of cells—yet all these are integrated by one head. It is true also in the Church: Jesus gives unity to His body.

d. He is the center of intelligence. The brain of the human body is located in the head. This marvelous organ directs all the functions and integrates all the systems of the body. Similarly, the "mind of Christ" must be the mind of the Church.

As a first general principle, then, we affirm that Jesus Christ is the Head of the Body and we must discern the operation of the triune Godhead within the Body.

2. *To carry out the will of the Head, the Holy Spirit works invisibly within the Body.* The Holy Spirit has been called the "executive of the Godhead." An executive is one who carries out the will of his superior by organizing the wills of those he guides.

What the Spirit does in the Church and in the churches would make an interesting study. In the enumeration of the gifts—they are called gifts of the *Spirit*—found in 1 Corinthians 12:4-13, the Spirit is mentioned nine times, the Son twice, and the Father once. "As they ministered to the Lord, and fasted, the Holy Ghost said, Separate me Barnabas and Saul for the work whereunto I have called them" (Acts 13:2). "Take heed therefore unto yourselves," said Paul to the Ephesian ministers, "and to all the flock, over the which the Holy Ghost hath made you overseers" (20:28). "He that hath an ear, let him hear what the Spirit saith unto the churches" (Revelation 2:11).

The Greek word for Spirit is the same as the one for the spirit of man. We may say that James' description of the human body is likewise a description of the body of Christ: "The body without the spirit is dead" (James 2:26).

3. *In the Church, as elsewhere in Christian human relations, members must practice submission of their personal rights to the welfare of the group.* There are times when one has a right to do something, but when it should not be done because it would hinder the functioning of the group.

Paul touched on this point several times in his letters, for example in Romans 14. In this helpful chapter Paul discusses the freedom that many have in the observance of days and in the eating of certain foods. His own personal conviction is stated in verse 14: "I know, and am persuaded by the Lord Jesus, that there is nothing unclean of itself: but to him that esteemeth any thing to be unclean, to him it is unclean." But because some new Christians do not yet have that knowledge, "It is good neither to eat flesh, nor to drink wine, nor any thing whereby thy brother stumbleth, or is offended, or is made weak" (v. 21). A similar discussion may be found in 1 Corinthians 8 and 9.

4. *Another Biblical principle of organization is the sovereignty of the local congregation.* Sovereignty means having supreme control. In the New Testament the highest form of organization is a council of local congregations deliberating together to determine the mind of the Lord. This council can recommend but not require. The churches who wish to remain within the confines of the council voluntarily agree to do so and demonstrate their desire by correspondence in doctrine and purpose and by general cooperation with other churches in the associated group.

Organizing Activities

The Early Church was simply too "early" to demand any elaborate form of organization. But as we read its records on the pages of the New Testament, we discover a surprising number of events betraying the fact of a beginning organization. Had not Jesus himself chosen the Twelve and put in their hands the control of the forthcoming Church? Did not this group have its own treasury and chief spokesman? How much more then the infant Church would need to create administrative devices and offices.

1. *Regular worship* (Acts 20:7; Hebrews 10:25). It appears that the first Christians met with undisturbed regularity for the specific purpose of worshiping God. This they did by means of a service involving the breaking of bread, prayer, Spirit-guided utterances, confession, and preaching. The Hebrews passage warns against "forsaking the assembling of ourselves together," thereby indicating this to be a regular and expected practice.

There were no church buildings as we know them in the New Testament Church. The idea of distinct buildings set apart for the purpose of Christian worship did not materialize till many years later. One reason for this was that Christianity, several centuries after its origin, came to be considered an illegal religion. During a later persecution by Rome, Christians—because they did not worship the gods recognized by the state—were even called atheists! Another reason there were no church buildings was the practice of the first Christians (most of whom were Jewish) of continuing to attend the temple services (Acts 2:46; 3:1; 5:12). Assemblies were held in homes (Philemon 2; Romans 16:5; 1 Corinthians 16:19; Colossians 4:15).

2. *Contributions* (Romans 15:26; 1 Corinthians 16:1, 2). A planned fund-raising campaign was going on in the Early Church. The saints at Jerusalem had undergone severe poverty in some instances, and Paul was anxious to provide them with financial as-

sistance. "Upon the first day of the week" is a good phrase to keep in mind when setting up a giving program. Second Corinthians 8 and 9 are the "giving chapters" in the New Testament.

3. *Social action* (1 Timothy 5:9; Acts 6:1). These passages show that the Church was concerned about its widows. There were enrollment lists of widows who received support (1 Timothy 5:9). Persons were carefully reviewed before they were enrolled. No "floaters" were allowed nor were insincere matrons tolerated. If relatives could support the widows, it was not right for the Church to do so (v. 16). It is entirely proper for the Church to care for its widows and retired ministers and to seek to meet the physical needs of other destitute people and in so doing serve Christ (Matthew 25:37-40).

4. *Ordination* (Acts 13:2, 3). The Holy Spirit calls men and women to the ministry. A church in its ordination service does not confer ordination so much as it recognizes it. The ordaining of ministers by a church visibly attests a previous divine ordination: "Separate me Barnabas and Saul for the work whereunto I have called them."

5. *Council* (15:6). The occasion of this first council of the Church was a specific doctrinal question: Must a person keep the Law to be saved (vv. 1, 2)? The matter was considered by the whole church—the apostles, the elders, and the brethren (vv. 22, 23). The decision was made by the brethren, but "it seemed good to the Holy Ghost, and to us" (v. 28). When they read the decision, the brethren "rejoiced for the consolation" (v. 31).

6. *Elections* (Acts 1:23-26; 6:5, 6). Both a replacement for Judas and a group of deacons were selected by elections. An interesting proverb in the Old Testament shows that God may work His will through such methods: "The lot is cast into the lap;

but the whole disposing thereof is of the LORD" (Proverbs 16:33).

The Ministry of the Church

One of the principles of Protestantism is the rediscovery of the priesthood of all believers. The separation of the body of Christ into the clergy and the laity sometimes overlooks this important principle. We all stand equal before God; we all are called to follow Christ; we all must be spiritual ministers whatever our vocations. We are all members of the Body and so have some function to perform.

While this is true, it is equally true that there are some members of the Body whose proper function is to spend their lives in direct service to the Body. What are these ministries?

1. *The apostle.* An apostle is one specifically commissioned to represent another. An ambassador is a political apostle, while a missionary is an ecclesiastical apostle. There were originally 12, although Judas was lost and Matthias and Paul were added. Special revelations and exceptional ministries seem to have been given these men. Modern apostles do organizing work that parallels that of the Twelve, but their labors do not have the same place in the foundation of the Church as the Twelve.

2. *The prophet.* In the Old Testament, these men were gifted speakers, often endowed with an array of prophetic and spiritual gifts related to utterance. In the New Testament the prophet ministered more directly to the assembly, doing so through exercising the gift of prophecy. The New Testament prophet should be distinguished from the Old Testament prophet. Agabus, Judas, and Silas were New Testament prophets (Acts 15:32; 21:10).

3. *The evangelist.* An evangelist is one who an-

nounces the good news of the gospel to all people. He is especially concerned with getting the lost to Christ, while the teacher is concerned with the instruction of babes in Christ. The pastor must oversee both evangelism and instruction in the congregation given him by God.

4. *The pastor-teacher.* The Greek of Ephesians 4:11 makes it clear that one office is referred to here by its two functions. The pastor has charge of the spiritual care of the congregation God has given him. That there were some teachers not associated with one particular congregation is clear from Acts 13:1 and Romans 12:7.

5. *The deacon.* These spiritual laymen were selected and even ordained to oversee business matters of the church (Acts 6:3, 6). But they also engaged in preaching, as the ministries of Stephen and Philip illustrate.

6. *Other ministries.* 1 Corinthians 12:28 and Romans 12:6-8 reveal that the ministry is not limited to the clergy. These other ministries were found in the congregation: *ministry,* in the sense of helpful service; *exhortation,* the encouragement of others; *ruling,* administrative oversight, whether of tiny committees or of entire denominations; *giving,* which should be recognized as a spiritual ministry; *showing mercy,* a service open to all; *miracles,* one of the gifts of the Spirit; and then a list including "healings, helps, governments, diversities of tongues." The important thing here is that each one may prayerfully determine his or her own ministry, then build it in the Lord.

The Membership of the Church

Twelve apostles; 3,000 members! The Church could not exist without lay persons. The ministry, in fact, serves this very purpose—to serve the masses of common people daily following the Lord.

Church membership in the New Testament was extended to those who had sincerely repented of their sins and had identified themselves with a group of worshiping Christians. They were persons who had followed the Lord in water baptism and who regularly shared in the Lord's Supper. They gave heed to their leaders by submitting themselves to Christ.

8
Destiny of the Church

"The Father of glory"—this is the lofty title Paul gives to God in his great letter about the Church (Ephesians 1:17). No purpose or act of man can be higher than to glorify God. "Whether therefore ye eat, or drink, or whatsoever ye do, do all to the glory of God" (1 Corinthians 10:31).

Glory, in the Biblical sense, means fame, praise, and honor arising from the majesty of royal rule. Think of the glory of the British sovereign. All glory, we learn in the Bible, both starts with and returns to the great God of all the earth.

In his letter to the Ephesians, Paul surveys the staggering purpose of God in uniting Jew and Gentile in one Body. Then he prays for understanding. And his thrilled heart bursts forth with praise for God: "Unto him be glory in the church!" (3:21).

"The heavens declare the glory of God"—and they do so not voluntarily but automatically (Psalm 19:1). It is in the Church, His own building, that God finds most glory. For nothing glorifies God so much as the song of the redeemed.

How the Church Glorifies God

What is the destiny of the Church? We discover that the Church is destined to give God glory here on earth. At the same time it is destined—not now, but later—to receive glory from God. So the Church glorifies God—that is its earthly destiny; and God glorifies the Church—that is its heavenly destiny.

The body of Christ on earth is the visible group of redeemed persons who walk the earth today giving glory to God. This statement is ideally true but not always actually true. Therefore, Paul urged the Thessalonians to walk worthy of God, who had called them unto His kingdom and glory (1 Thessalonians 2:12).

There are two major ways the Church glorifies God. Expressed in two words, they are *evangelism* and *edification*—these are the work of the Church.

God's Glory Through Evangelism

1. *God wishes to be glorified.* He is a Person, a divine Person. He expects praise: "Give unto the Lord the glory due unto his name; worship the Lord in the beauty of holiness" (Psalm 29:2). "Honor and majesty are before him: strength and beauty are in his sanctuary. Give unto the LORD, O ye kindreds of the people, give unto the LORD glory and strength" (96:6, 7).

As a jealous God, He demanded in the first commandment: "Thou shalt have no other gods before me" (Exodus 20:3). Through the prophet Isaiah He asserts: "I will not give my glory unto another" (Isaiah 48:11).

2. *God wills all men to be saved* (2 Peter 3:9). God wills all to be saved because the salvation of a person brings highest glory to His name. The state of sin is defined by the Bible as coming "short of the glory of God" (Romans 3:23). Repentance and conversion, therefore, secure the fulfillment of the glory of God in the life of an individual.

3. *Jesus taught that heaven rejoices when one is*

saved. Notice the tender story of the shepherd seeking the one lost sheep. The Great Shepherd of the souls of men is continually seeking the straying lamb. Luke 15:7, 10 informs us of the jubilation in heaven in the presence of the angels when one sinner repents. By winning men the Church brings glory to God and brings about heavenly happiness.

4. *Accepting Christ reverses the effects of the Fall.* One is not taken immediately to heaven upon repentance and confession. There is an aspect to salvation that awaits the Second Coming for fulfillment (Luke 21:28; Romans 13:11; 1 Peter 1:5). Yet in conversion the downward tilt in the heart of man is offset with the introduction of a new life within. So you could say the Fall is countered in conversion with the Rise—the beginning of a sanctified life bringing glory to God.

5. *The destiny of the Church in the present age is to add to the body of Christ those who believe.* By doing this, the Church is glorifying God. It is doing so even by increasing the volume of praise going up to God in the lives of more and more who are led to faith.

In summary, to bring the lost to God is the present mission of the Church. Evangelism is the present destiny of the Church; for this purpose it was formed. For every single soul led to God produces happiness in heaven. The glory is God's but it is secured for Him both in and by the Church. Remember why King Herod died an awful death? "Because he gave not God the glory" (Acts 12:23).

God's Glory Through Edification

The first way the Church brings glory to God, and thereby fulfills its present destiny, is by evangelizing the lost. The second way it does this is by edifying itself. It must get the gospel both out and in—out to the world of lost men, and into the hearts of saved men.

1. *The word "edify" means to build up, to establish, to improve, to instruct.* Looking inward, the Church must build itself up by advancing its members spiritually. "Let all things be done unto edifying" (1 Corinthians 14:26) is a rule that relates not only to the gifts of the Spirit but also to the collective activities of the assembled Church and to the individual behavior of each member.

Hear the Scripture passages on edification: "Let us therefore follow after the things which make for peace, and things wherewith one may edify another" (Romans 14:19). "Let every one of us please his neighbor for his good to edification" (15:2). Twice in 2 Corinthians Paul contrasts the power given him by the Lord for edification with its other possible use—destruction (10:8; 13:10). "Charity [love] edifieth" (1 Corinthians 8:1). After they had become convinced of the reality of Paul's conversion, "Then had the churches rest throughout all Judea and Galilee and Samaria, and were edified" (Acts 9:31).

Perhaps the most direct Biblical statement about the edifying task of the Church is that given in Ephesians 4:12, where among the reasons given for God's gifts to the Church of the ministerial offices is this one: "For the edifying of the body of Christ."

2. *Believers enter the Church as spiritual babies.* They come in by way of a new birth (John 3:5). They need the "sincere milk of the word" (1 Peter 2:2). They must not be allowed to remain in spiritual infancy but must be nourished and fed in order to grow up to perfect manhood, fashioned after the image of Christ (Romans 8:29; Ephesians 4:13). The constant goal of the Bible for its followers is spiritual maturity.

3. *The local church must be what the universal Church is—a sheepfold where nourishment is provided for the flock.* Again consult Ephesians 4:12, which tells why God gave ministers to the Church. Not one of the reasons listed relates primarily to lost men. The apostle, the prophet, the evangelist, the teaching pastor—all were given to the Church. Their purpose is to serve this Church, to nourish it.

We have imagined that ministers are the paid witnesses whose task it is to proclaim the gospel. But that is the task of the entire Church, of every member in it, and not merely of ministers. These were given rather to that witnessing Body to guide it in its work. When the Church is rightly fed by its ministers, its servants (that is what the word *minister* means), it will be a witnessing Church.

4. *How does the Church edify itself?* Many ways could be listed. They would include the following: (1) public worship, on regular days; (2) the preaching and exposition of God's Word; (3) sharing in the Lord's Supper; (4) encouraging private devotional habits among its members; (5) employment of the gifts of the Spirit, which are calculated to edify; and (6) developing total stewardship of means and time.

This, then, is the destiny of the Church for the present time: to evangelize the lost and to edify the saved; to get converts and to keep them. In performing this work of the Church the body of Christ brings glory to its Lord. In the winning and teaching Church the Lord receives "glory in the church."

How God Will Glorify the Church

The present time, before the coming of the Lord, is the period when the Church is glorifying its Lord by carrying out the work assigned to it. By contrast, it is in the future, following the coming of the Lord, when the Church will receive its glory. For we await the wholeness of history to experience all God has in mind for the Church. While the Church *now* glorifies God, God will *then* glorify the Church.

It is also true that the future of the Church is the future of its individual members. This is true because the Church is simply an entire Body of members. The future of the Church is a very different thing from the future of a denomination. Denominations may tumble and decay—even die. But the church of God never fails. "The gates of hell shall not prevail against it" (Matthew 16:18).

How will God glorify the Church?

Judgment on the World

1. *The same world the Church evangelizes, God judges.* That world of fallen men is already standing under judgment—they are "condemned already.... And this is the condemnation, that light is come into the world, and men loved darkness rather than light, because their deeds were evil" (John 3:18, 19).

Yet the full and final judgment of those who already stand condemned awaits the coming of the Lord. This is a sobering thought. The Lord will come with glory for some but with judgment for others. The returning Lord will bring "tribulation" for the wicked and "rest" for the saved (2 Thessalonians 1:6, 7).

2. *Judgment involves separation.* God will glorify the Church in the day of judgment by extracting from it all pretenders and all evil. This evil and these evil persons will be banished forever from the presence of God, which is the promised inheritance of the saints. We are not able to fully understand all the workings of eternity. But there is comfort in the

verse: "Enter thou into the joy of thy lord" (Matthew 25:23).

3. *Christians experience God's judgment now; the world will experience it later.* Our judgment is for purification; theirs is for damnation. "But when we are judged, we are chastened of the Lord, that we should not be condemned with the world" (1 Corinthians 11:32). "Judgment must begin at the house of God" (1 Peter 4:17). There is no question as to whether or not all men shall be judged of the Lord. The question is, "When?" Strange as it may sound, God is glorifying the Church by judging it now so it may escape the last judgment.

Perfection in the Church

1. *The future of the Church includes its perfection in knowledge, number, and holiness by God.* It is God, after all, who adds to the Church those who are saved: "And believers were the more added to the Lord, multitudes both of men and women" (Acts 5:14). Elsewhere, Luke reverses his manner of speaking: "And the Lord added to the church daily such as should be saved" (2:47). There will come a time when the body of Christ will be complete in number. We know too that after we reach heaven we shall know as we are known, and we shall join "the spirits of just men made perfect" (1 Corinthians 13:12; Hebrews 12:23).

2. *While the world of unbelieving men will be separated from God, we who believe will be separated to God.* In heaven there will be no shadows for the Lamb is the light. "No night there" is not an idle dream but a Biblical hope. We simply cannot imagine the things God has prepared for them that believe. The best we can understand is to call it a new heaven and a new earth.

3. *Meanwhile, the Church—as each individual member—carries with its earthly walk the sure promise of perfection.* "He which hath begun a good work in you will perform it until the day of Jesus Christ" (Philippians 1:6). "The Lord will perfect that which concerneth me" (Psalm 138:8).

This, then, is the double destiny of the church of Christ. On earth it mirrors the glory of God by getting God's will done in the hearts of men. It does this by evangelism and by edification. In heaven it will be crowned with glory by the "Father of glory" (Ephesians 1:17), when in a stroke He matures the Church to perfection and divides from it those forever condemned to imperfection.

9

The Early Church

All the chapters up to now have been concerned with the *theology* of the Church. We turn now to the *history* of the Church. The institution Jesus founded was not a dreamer's idea; it became concrete reality. It consists of actual deeds of real men and women done in our world. The Church of the New Testament has continued through history right down to today. Here, in the remaining chapters of this book, is a short survey of the history of the Church.

"History is a seamless garment," someone has well said. Like the cloak of Jesus, history does not have precise dividing lines. The historical periods overlap, and only approximate divisions are appropriate. Here is a list of periods and dates that form the basis of these chapters (all dates are A.D.):

Early Church	30-600
Medieval Church	600-1300
Reformation	1300-1600
Early Modern Church	1600-1900
Twentieth Century	1900 to date

Life in the Roman Empire

The world of the Early Church, of which the New Testament Church was the beginning, was a Roman world. In succession the empires of Egypt,

Babylonia, Assyria, Persia, and Greece had risen and fallen. Now Rome ruled the world. By the time Jesus came to earth the Roman Empire had put to an end the many wars throughout the Mediterranean world and secured a general unity of men. Indeed, this very fact is one evidence that God sent forth His Son "in the fullness of ... time" (Galatians 4:4).

The Roman Empire was a model of statehood. It provided an unprecedented era of peace and justice. The Romans were builders, and they stretched out a network of roads shortly to be traveled by the great apostle Paul in his missionary journeys. Some of these roads were so well constructed they can be seen today.

The culture of the period, however, was a gift of the Greeks who had been superseded by the Romans. Art, sculpture, athletics, literature—the ideals in these areas came from the Greeks.

Also the language of the Greeks dominated the Roman world, although Latin was spoken in some sections. The New Testament was written in Greek, even though most of its authors were Jews. Already by Jesus' time, the Old Testament had been translated from Hebrew into the widely used Greek of the period.

Rome was ruled by emperors, the majority of whom were hostile to Christianity. This new religion was at first viewed as a sect of the Jews, but it soon made clear its severance from that group.

The emperors demanded worship of themselves, since Romans believed in the divinity of the state. One could have any religion, so long as he paid proper respect to the emperor by bowing before his image. True Christians, of course, could not do this.

After A.D. 400 the Roman Empire decayed, having first reached the place where Christianity had become the official state religion.

The political unity, the common language, the era of peace, and spiritual hunger paved the way for the spread of the gospel.

Trends in the Early Church

Within the first 5 or 6 centuries of the history of the Church a number of important trends appeared. These trace effectively the course of the Church in that time. Let us look at them.

1. *The expansion of the Church.* From its start Christianity was a missionary Church. Antioch became a prominent missionary center. From it Paul began his first missionary journey (Acts 13:1-4). Before Antioch, Jerusalem had been the center. After Antioch outstanding metropolises of the Roman world became jumping-off points for Christian missions. These included Ephesus, where Paul spent some time, and Alexandria, the gateway to Africa.

In its prime the Roman Empire stretched from England to Arabia. And wherever Rome was, there was the gospel witness. Justin Martyr, one of the Church fathers who lived in the second century, could already write:

> There is no people, Greek or Barbarian, or any other race, by whatsoever appellation or manner they may be distinguished, . . . among whom prayers and thanksgivings are not offered, in the name of the crucified Jesus, to the Father and creator of all things (Justin Martyr, *Dialogue With Trypho*, p. 117).

At first persecuted, Christianity moved with such speed and success it soon could no longer be ignored. After a final wave of persecution, a striking thing happened. There went forth from the Roman emperor the famed Edict of Milan in which Christianity became a legal religion. This happened in

313. By 395 Christianity was made the official religion of the entire empire.

2. *The completion of the Bible.* While the Church was busy expanding, God provided authoritative literature to define the contents of the Christian message. Jesus himself had set the pattern for recognizing and quoting heavily an authoritative religious Book. "All things must be fulfilled," He said in Luke 24:44, "which were written in the law of Moses, and in the prophets, and in the psalms, concerning me."

While Jesus himself wrote no book, His disciples and their associates—not more than nine in all—were inspired by the Holy Spirit to write the 27 Books of the New Testament between A.D. 50 and 100. Yet these were not all immediately received as God's Word. It took time for churches on one side of the empire even to receive the Books, some of which were to be read to churches other than the ones addressed. (See Colossians 4:16.) Besides, many fake gospels circulated in the name of the apostles, as if written by them.

Gradually the Church came to recognize which ones God had intended to form a New Testament to be placed beside the Old. The periods in this process of recognizing the canon of Scripture have been summarized by W. H. Griffith Thomas *(The Principle of Theology* [London: Church Book Room Press, 1956], p. 111):

A.D.	50-100	composing, writing
A.D.	100-200	collecting, gathering
A.D.	200-300	comparing, sifting
A.D.	300-400	completing, recognizing

3. *The formalization of worship.* While the life of the Church was being spread by some, it was becoming crystallized by others. Wherever heartfelt reli-

gious experience fades, the tendency arises to solidify a fixed pattern of worship. This tendency grew in the second century and increased rapidly thereafter. Some began to consider the Lord's Supper as a repetition of the sacrifice of Calvary. Offering the Lord's Supper as a sacrifice from week to week became the foundation of the Roman Catholic doctrine of the Mass to be developed later.

Similarly, baptism was soon considered as possessing in itself the power of regeneration. Children were baptized and when they were of age, "confirmed." Choirs were used much more, and liturgical forms of worship became standardized. Preaching declined. The minister became a priest, an intercessor who would offer the sacrifice of the Mass, rather than one on the same level as the congregation. This, of course, forced a wedge between the clergy and the laity and foreshadowed the corruption that was to develop, finally erupting into the Reformation. In the same period emerged the first monks who, all too often in their getting out of the sinful world, failed to get the sinful world out of themselves.

4. *The exaltation of the Roman bishop.* When Christianity was but a small movement, it could be governed by the apostles from Jerusalem. After the apostles died and the Church expanded all over the empire, it became necessary to set up administrative points geographically distributed. Thus, Alexandria cared for Egypt, and Constantinople for Asia Minor. In the western part of the Mediterranean area, Rome, the capital of the empire, became the natural administrative point.

As time passed and the Church grew still larger, the bishop of Rome began to assume an administrative superiority. This was natural enough, since the city of Rome was the capital city of the empire. By this time, bishops had become a separate and higher office than elders or overseers. In the New Testament they seem to be different terms for one office. The tradition had developed that Peter, the one on whom Jesus had said He would found His church, was the first bishop of Rome. (That Peter was ever in Rome is still disputed.) His successors became viewed as continuing the supposed authority given him by Christ. Thus was born the office of the pope.

In this period the Church was still one church, although we are able to observe in seed-form the tendencies that would in the next centuries lead to Roman Catholicism. But that is a later development. At this time the Church was truly catholic, in the sense of being universal; located throughout the entire world and being an unbroken unit.

Early Christian Fathers

Israel had its fathers (Hebrews 1:1) and so did the early Christians (1 Corinthians 4:15). Fathers are the respected pioneers of any group. The Church fathers are those many men who in the early years of the Christian Church lent their consecrated talents to the founding, establishment, and especially the defense of the youthful Church. Here are some of them.

1. *Justin Martyr—The Philosopher* (100-165). This brilliant Greek was permitted the luxury of leisurely study, since Justin Martyr was born of wealthy parents. A serious lad, he sought the answer to life's problems in the study of philosophy, several varieties of which he embraced in turn. Following a life-changing challenge given when an old man asked how philosophers could know anything about a God they had never seen or heard, he gave his life to God and to the Church. Never an official officeholder, he retained the traditional cloak worn by philosophers as a mark of distinction and utilized

philosophical ideas to defend Christianity. His example shows that the gospel also appeals to the educated.

2. *Tertullian—The Lawyer* (150-220). Son of a Roman centurion, this civil servant of the Roman state became a Christian near the age of 40. Unlike Justin, Tertullian had little use for philosophy. His mind, well-trained in law, was the source of many well-put defenses of Christianity during the period when it was an illegitimate religion. It was Tertullian who first applied the words *New Testament* to the 27 Books we call by that name.

3. *Origen—The Theologian* (185-254). The son of a Christian, Origen was well-trained in the literature of the classical world and in the Scriptures. In the opinion of A. Souter, Origen was "the greatest Biblical scholar who ever lived" *(The Text and Canon of the New Testament* [London: Duckworth, 1954], p. 159). He is said to have written 6,000 books, pamphlets, letters, and other writings. He prepared the *Hexapla,* a careful edition of the Old Testament in Hebrew and several types of Greek. Some say his quotations from the New Testament in his writings reached the staggering figure of 18,000. He is an example of the Biblical scholar without whose aid we would not have our modern English versions.

4. *Jerome—The Translator* (340-420). To prepare a version of the Bible in Latin so the Latin-speaking peoples could read God's Word, Jerome went to Palestine from his home in Rome and studied Hebrew for 5 years. He produced the Latin translation called *The Vulgate,* which for 1,000 years was the official Bible of the Church and is still recognized as such by the Roman Catholic Church.

The translation of the Bible into other languages continues and in January 1977 some part of the Scriptures appeared in 1603 languages. "Faith cometh by hearing, and hearing by the word of God" (Romans 10:17).

5. *Augustine—The Teacher* (354-430). Augustine poured his training as a teacher into the Church following his conversion after reading Romans 13:13, 14. *The Confessions of St. Augustine* is a devotional classic. Augustine said: "Thou madest us for Thyself, and our heart is restless until it repose in Thee" *(Confessions,* 1.1).

6. *Chrysostom—The Preacher* (347-407). Called the "golden-throated orator," Chrysostom was the greatest expositor in the eastern Church. One of his slogans fits today: "This is the cause of all our evils, our not knowing the Scriptures."

Persecutions

At first Christianity was protected by the Roman state (Acts 18:14-16). When its rapid growth produced a sizable following of persons unwilling to bow before the emperor, the disregard turned to concern lest the empire be threatened.

Why were the Christians persecuted? There are several reasons. While the Romans were tolerant of any religion, the worshiper must not decline to do sacrifice to the emperor. So long as he would do this he could follow any other religion. The Christians refused to do this and so were charged—curiously—with being atheists, since they would not recognize the Roman gods embodied in the state and would not participate in the ceremonies of the state religion. Also, most of the Christians were common people, lower in status than the cultured Romans.

Historians usually count 10 waves of persecution occurring between the years A.D. 64 and 303. In the first, Peter and Paul are thought to have suffered martyrdom.

A letter of inquiry from a governor assigned to a province of Asia Minor, dated about A.D. 110, gives us some details about how the Christians were taken. Governor Pliny wrote to Emperor Trajan to ask if he should dispose of Christians just because they bore that name, or whether he should catch them in some crime. Trajan replied that Christians were to be punished just for being Christians. Characteristic of Roman tolerance, the law provided acquittal if one would renounce his past identification as a Christian and would worship a statue of the emperor brought into court for that purpose.

The brutal details of savage tortures to which the Christian martyrs were put are well known. A single example taken from the records of a famous Roman historian named Tacitus will illustrate the severity and injustice of the persecutions. Writing of the first persecution, which occurred under Nero (emperor from A.D. 54 to A.D. 68), Tacitus speaks of Nero's transfer of guilt from himself to the Christians concerning a great fire in Rome:

> First those were seized who confessed they were Christians.... And in their deaths they were also made the subject of sport, for they were covered with the hides of wild beasts, and worried to death by dogs, or nailed to crosses, or set fire to, and when day declined, were burned to serve for nocturnal lights. Nero offered his own gardens for that spectacle... *(Annals, 15.44. 5-7).*

Persecution of this dimension drove the Christians underground, where they met in secret. As a Christian sign they used the sign of a fish, because the letters of the Greek word for fish form the initials of the Greek title "Jesus Christ, Son of God, Saviour."

There were other effects of the persecutions. One requirement of an accused Christian was to surrender any copies of the Scriptures he might have in his possession. This meant the destruction of thousands of handmade copies of the Scriptures and accounts somewhat for the lack of full agreement among existing manuscript copies.

But the greatest effect of the persecutions was no doubt the separation it made between the wholehearted Christians and the fainthearted. This is the abiding spiritual lesson: God uses persecution to purify faith.

10
The Medieval Church

The thousand years stretching from roughly A.D. 500 to 1500 are the middle years of Christian history. They have been called, in secular history, the Dark Ages because of the overall lack of forward motion in most areas. The same period is frequently termed the Medieval Age or Middle Ages.

During this period, the Church ceased to function as an organism and crystallized into an organization. The persecuted but spiritually thriving Church of the earliest centuries in this period attained such ecclesiastical and even political strength that it actually dominated the history of the period. Consult any standard history of the world and you will discover the history of the Western world is to a large extent the history of the Church.

Here began the church-state relationships so important today. At first disregarded, the Church was successively tolerated, persecuted, liberated, and finally enthroned by the state. The state, which once persecuted the Church, was now swallowed up by it.

The Medieval World

With the arrival of A.D. 476, the fall of the once-glorious Roman Empire was complete. The next 1,000 years would see a cleavage between the East and the West. Wars of varying results and importance would break out, and solidarity in the West would await the 11th century.

Even before the fall of Rome, the empire had been split. Interest and importance shifted to the eastern city of Constantinople in northwestern Asia Minor.

Constantinople became the center of a new empire—the Byzantine—which dominated the area of Asia Minor and Greece with changing forcefulness until the coming of the Turks in 1453.

What was left of the Roman Empire was squeezed between two jaws—the barbarian tribes in the north and the Moslem fanatics in the south all across the northern coast of Africa. In this western area, covering the territory now known as Italy, Switzerland, Germany, and into the Scandinavian countries and the British Isles, the "Holy Roman Empire" arose. Some historians point out that this kingdom was neither holy nor Roman nor an empire.

The feudal system predominated. The common man would attach himself to a wealthy lord who, in exchange for military service and stipulated payments of taxes, would protect the property rights and the welfare of his underlings. It was the age of knights and ladies. Boys lived for the time when they would be knighted. Such a system induced class differences, which later were a source of social unrest.

From the north the Vikings swept down over England and raided the coasts of Europe, reaching into the Mediterranean.

While Europe went through stabilizing refinements, the nations of the Far East moved forward in civilization. India witnessed a golden age in its cultural development. China continued the cultural development that had been unbroken for so many centuries. Military strength and a divine regard for the emperor marked medieval Japan. Tales of travels in the Far East awakened Europe to the civilization that lay to its east.

The welding together of church and state was witnessed in the Crusades—military missions with at least a stated religious purpose.

In the 14th century came a rebirth of knowledge called the Renaissance. The glories of the ancient classical world, of the Greco-Roman Empire, were rediscovered through translation of its best documents. The Arabs especially had preserved learning through the dark years, and had absorbed certain developments from the Far East. From them we have the symbol *zero* and our decimal system of numbering.

The great universities were born during this period. Lengthy programs were set up for study, especially in the fields of law, theology, and medicine.

In literature the Italian Dante gave the world a popular expression of theology in *The Divine Comedy*. In England Chaucer produced the *Canterbury Tales*.

Little happened in science, for all discoveries had to conform to the teachings of the church. Roger Bacon, however, emphasized the inductive method of reasoning, an important tool of later science.

The mariner's compass and the rudder made sailing more venturous and foreshadowed an age of exploration.

Huge Gothic cathedrals, some remaining to this day, attested to the genius and patience of the age.

The Rise of the Roman Catholic Church

The catholic Church of the early centuries of Christian history increasingly throughout the Middle Ages became the Roman Catholic Church. Protestants did not object to the idea of a "catholic" Church, for the world *catholic* means universal. Their opposition focused on the decayed spirituality and embellished formalism that developed within the church.

The Papacy

Doubtless one of the strongest reasons for the rise of Romanism was the increasingly dominant role played by the pope.

What elevated the importance of the pope? The answer is complex. The supposed rule of Peter in Rome was interpreted as God's will for the Roman bishop to have preeminence over the other bishops of the Christian world. These popes resembled the kings of Israel in one respect—some walked after the evil manners of their fathers; some were righteous men. It is a mistake to suppose every pope was a rascal.

Furthermore, the eastern part of the Roman Empire had been inching away from the West ever since the days of Emperor Constantine, who moved the capital from Rome to Constantinople in Asia Minor. This meant the civil ruler, the emperor, sat in Constantinople; while the highest church official sat in Rome—several hundred miles to the West. So when the Roman Empire crumbled and the eastern part crystallized into the Byzantine Empire, the pope was left holding the pieces, so to speak, of the broken empire. It was to be expected, therefore, that the religious leader would assume some political leadership as well.

This temporal, civil ruling power assumed by the pope heightened the importance of the office. His influence grew through the missionary expansion of the church to the barbaric peoples. The missionary labored under orders to attach evangelized lands to the Roman pontiff. When the entire political unity and religious freedom of the church was threatened by the invading Moslems, the faithful rallied round the pope and sought his protection.

Besides these natural factors which account for the rise of the papal office, there were occasional falsehoods spread abroad among the unsuspecting public. One of these was called the "Donation of Constantine." It spread the erroneous idea that Emperor Constantine had given the bishop of Rome and his successors supreme authority over the provinces of Europe, and the reason the emperor had moved the capital away from Rome was to avoid creating a rival to the pope.

Another fake document was known as the "False Decretals of Isidore." This writing allegedly recorded the opinions of the early Roman bishops that the Roman bishops were totally sovereign, the clergy were exempt from any responsibility to the state, and no court could judge a priest.

After the desired effects had been created, these documents were discovered to be forgeries. Yet the office of the pope had so arisen that by the end of the 12th century, Pope Innocent III not only ruled sovereignly over the church but also kept a strong hand over the entire extent of the revived Roman Empire stretching through central and northern Europe. Today, while his earthly rule is not so extensive, the pope has a hand in widely scattered nations giving their allegiance to him on account of their commitment to the Roman Catholic faith.

The East-West Split

The division of the empire was foreshadowed by Constantine in his transfer of the capital. Such a division was strengthened by the racial difference between the Greek-speaking people of the East and the Latin-speaking people of the West. No small rivalry existed between the two.

First, the eastern church ruler, who is known as a patriarch, through an assembled council deposed the pope. Then in a final breach the pope denounced the patriarch. This occurred in A.D. 1054, and marked the separation of the Christian Church into two major divisions—the western Roman Catholic Church and the eastern Greek Orthodox Church. Both have continued to this day.

Success and Failure in the Medieval Church

Both must be seen in the medieval church. On the side of success, it was the church that kept alive the light of the gospel through the dark period. It evangelized the barbarian tribes of Europe, however inadequate that evangelism was. In this regard, the medieval church passed on Paul's initial thrust into Europe and accounted for the Christianity of the Western world.

In addition, the medieval church exerted a unifying influence on the broken states of Europe, helping to achieve some political unity necessary for the continued existence of the continent. Learning was preserved by the church to a large degree. Monks in monasteries had become notorious and is probably classical works and reproducing them by hand. Not to be overlooked is the work done in copying the Scriptures. Had the church not preserved and passed on the Scriptures, the barbarian world certainly would not have been concerned with this task.

On the failure side of the medieval church, the score is heavy. The corruption of the clergy and the monasteries has become notorious and is probably perceived out of proportion to other ills. One such is the laziness and greed resulting from the bulging wealth of the church. The failure of the clergy resulted in the neglect of the people; masses were left without true shepherds. This in turn dropped the level of religion and produced a vacuum in spirituality. The low point reached was soon to be jolted by the bold, protesting reformers.

The Emergence of Islam

1. *The man.* Mohammed was born at Mecca, in Arabia, in A.D. 570. He died in A.D. 632. Influenced early by the Jewish religion, his faith still shows the effects of Jewish theology. At the age of 40, Mohammed began preaching the simple creed: "There is no God but Allah, and Mohammed is His prophet." ("Allah" comes from a word related to the Hebrew word for God.) His preaching gained converts and brought such persecution that in 622 he was forced to flee the city. This flight became the starting point of the Mohammedan calendar. All Arabia heard his message before he died.

2. *The message.* Mohammed taught a simple faith. God is one, and is not represented by pictures or images such as the Greeks were accustomed to making. This God foreordains all that comes to pass. The events of the world are viewed fatalistically, as if they happen without reference to the actions of man. There is not a deep conception of sin in Islam, and neither is there much place for forgiveness by grace. Heaven is a sensual place, not a spiritual one. The *Koran* is the holy book of the Moslem. Of the prophets God sent to man, Adam, Moses, and Jesus were next-best to Mohammed.

3. *The meaning.* The significance of Islam for Christianity can be seen from the extent of its con-

quests. The Moslem's tool was the sword; by the sword he lived and conquered. The Arabians were the fierce sons of Ishmael. By the time of Mohammed's death, Arabia had been conquered. By A.D. 900 his followers had surged north and west, occupying the lands in Palestine, Syria, Egypt, North Africa, Spain, and other parts of Europe.

In the famous Battle of Tours in A.D. 732, the sweeping hordes of Moslem conquerors were halted and Europe was saved from their control. "But for the Battle of Tours, it is possible that all Europe might have been a Mohammedan continent, and the crescent have taken the place of the cross." Thus concludes Jesse Lyman Hurlbut in *The Story of the Christian Church* (Philadelphia: Winston, 1954, p. 117).

4. *The Crusades.* One of the more dramatic features of the Middle Ages was the series of holy wars known as the Crusades. There were at least eight of them stretching over 200 years, between the 11th and 13th centuries.

The occasion of the Crusades was the Moslem conquest of the Holy Land. Ever since the ascension of Jesus, Christians had made unhindered pilgrimages to the sacred sights, as is still done today. Interest in this area increased with the coming of the year A.D. 1000, which many thought would bring the end of the world. Although the Mohammedans had occupied the Holy Land since the eighth century at least, Christians had been permitted to visit their sacred sights. Difficulty arose, however, when the Seljuk Turks took over the Holy Land from their fellow Moslem religionists who were Arabians. The Turks were fierce and intolerant and refused the Christians permission to enter the sacred city.

Seeing the Holy Land in the hands of the Mohammedans inflamed the religious passions of the European Christians. In 1095, Pope Urban II issued a call for a Christian army to hasten to the Holy Land to upend the Turks. This First Crusade was a glowing success. Three thousand knights with 12,000 infantrymen drove out the Turks and secured the release of Jerusalem.

Successive Crusades were not as purely motivated nor were they as successful. One of the famous ones was called the Children's Crusade, in which hundreds of children were sold into slavery by unscrupulous masters. As the Crusade movement gathered force, mixed motives prevailed. Shipping merchants charged exorbitant fares to reach the eastern Mediterranean shores. Thieves and debtors joined the movement to escape those who sought them. The church offered volunteers immunity from taxes and care of property, and many went merely to secure these benefits. And, of course, there were adventurers who went along for the ride.

Yet the Crusades had some definite results. The Holy Land was reopened to Christian pilgrims. The Moslems, however, regained all the territory that had been won and temporarily held by the Christian Crusaders. The frequent crossings of the Mediterranean stimulated commerce and brought about cultural interchange. Port cities expanded.

All in all, the downward spiritual drift of the church during the medieval period, when it excelled in other respects—culture, wealth, influence—warns against evaluating spiritual development by material prosperity.

11
The Reformation

If history is a "seamless garment," no single date can be cited as the precise origin of the Reformation. The nailing of Luther's famed "Ninety-five Theses" to the door of the Wittenberg church is as good a start as any. That happened on October 31, 1517. But things stirred long before that time; it was then they erupted.

Resentment of church ownership of large tracts of European lands, newly discovered possibilities in scientific achievement, opposition to the distance the church had put between teaching and practice, and indignation over the moral degradation of society—all these factors sparked the Reformation. But the straw that broke the camel's back was no doubt the bold sale of indulgences, by which the church offered (as perceived by some) permission to sin for a price.

It is difficult to decide whether Protestantism should be termed a *reformation* or a *revolt*. Although Luther died in the hope that the one existing church might be reformed, his followers were forced out of the church and their movement took the shape of a revolt. That the visible community of the body of Christ became spiritually revitalized warrants the title *Reformation*.

The World of the Reformation

At the outbreak of the Protestant Reformation, three nations dominated Europe. The most powerful was Spain, ruled over by Charles V. France had Francis I as its monarch, a strong rival to Charles V. In England Henry VIII reigned with abiding resentment against the papal claims on his country. Germany was then not a well-unified land, it was still "The Holy Roman Empire." The Turks who had taken Constantinople in 1453, became the enemies of Charles V. This political unrest was not an insignificant factor in the events of the Reformation.

It was a period of intellectual and scientific growth. The years A. D. 1350 to 1650 (which more than embrace the period of the Reformation) constitute the birth of the modern era in many fields, including politics, philosophy, religion, and science.

No single discovery contributed more to the modern period than the invention of printing about A.D. 1450. The first printed book is generally believed to have been the Bible. The printing press made it possible to eliminate the errors likely to arise from hand copies, to say nothing of the expense saved in reproducing books. Before printing in the Middle Ages, a copy of the Bible might cost a year's wages.

Printing tied in with the "Revival of Learning," the Renaissance. Throwing off the shackles of church authority, men shelved medieval superstitions and began serious scientific experimentation.

Copernicus, the astronomer, advanced the then unheard-of view (actually a revived Greek theory) that the sun and not the earth is the center of the universe. A contemporary of Luther and of the artist Michelangelo, Copernicus met with wide opposition to his theory of a sun-centered universe.

Some years later Galileo constructed a telescope

and confirmed the theory of Copernicus. Such a novel theory was opposed not only by the Roman Catholic Church, which forced Galileo to retract his arguments, but by men like Luther, Calvin, Shakespeare, Milton, and Francis Bacon.

The idea that the world was round like a sphere encouraged the exploration of the period. Columbus, as we know, reached the North American continent in 1492. Magellan sailed around the world, beginning his voyage in 1519.

By 1607, Jamestown had been settled in the New World, and America was on its way into existence.

In literature the incomparable Shakespeare wrote his classics and became more widely quoted than anyone outside of the Bible. Milton gave us *Paradise Lost* and Bunyan produced—in prison—*The Pilgrim's Progress*. Both men were Puritans. In 1611 the beloved King James Version of the Bible was produced.

In mathematics, John Napier published a work on logarithms in 1614 and paved the way for the invention of the slide rule 8 years later. In 1645 the first adding machine was invented.

In medicine, Harvey demonstrated the circulation of the blood, opening the way to medical and surgical advance.

Michelangelo sculpted, and Rembrandt painted.

Then came the microscope and the telescope, the thermometer and the barometer, the pendulum clock and the air pump.

The world was ripe for the Reformation of religion about to burst into existence.

The Protestant Reformation was not a single movement under the leadership of a single powerful personality. It was spread over the continent of Europe and the British Isles. The chief countries in which the Reformation progressed can be linked with outstanding leaders within them. Thus we will observe the Reformation era of the history of the Church biographically.

John Wycliffe and England

Born in 1320, John Wycliffe preceded Luther by over a century and a half. He is remembered as "the morning star of the Reformation." By his bold efforts and strong influence he smoothed the road for the forthcoming surge of Protestantism.

John Wycliffe was an exceptional scholar at Oxford University. Much of his life was spent teaching there after he received a doctor of theology degree from that famous school.

Wycliffe's opposition to Rome took the form of his stand against the tribute the pope yearly exacted from the English nation. He began to deny the doctrine of transubstantiation, the official explanation of the Mass which states that the wine and the bread actually change into the literal body and blood of Christ. Condemned by a church council, he boldly asserted the superiority of the Scriptures to the church as an ultimate source of recognized authority. In 1382 he was forced to leave the city for a country retirement.

In 1380 Wycliffe published the New Testament of what came to be the first complete Bible in the English language. This was before the invention of printing. He founded a group of lay preachers, the Lollards, who honeycombed England with Wycliffe's version, tracts, and sermons.

As a forerunner of the Reformation and as an exponent of Biblical religion in England, he contributed toward the Protestant leanings of that country. His Bible, completed with the publication of the Old

Testament in 1384, the year of his death, was the only one in English for 145 years.

Martin Luther and Germany

Most famous among the men of the Reformation, Martin Luther was a sincere man of strong moral conviction and a seeking heart. He was born of humble peasants, though his father worked his way into some small wealth in the copper mines. In spite of a university education Luther retained the superstitions common to his age, such as belief in witches.

After some short-lived interest in training as a lawyer, Luther sought answers to spiritual questions by entering a monastery of the Augustinian order. He received counsel there that was to guide his entire life. A superior recognized his inner struggles and urged him to trust God and consult the Scriptures. He soon turned a temporary appointment as professor of theology into a permanent one at the newly formed University of Wittenberg. From that post, Luther did his work as a reformer.

Luther began his activities as a priest of the church he was soon to divide. His interest was not in dividing the church, but in purifying it. He never relinquished the hope of seeing the Catholic Church reformed.

Pope Leo X, in office during Luther's time, needed more funds to complete the construction of the magnificent and elaborate capital of Catholicism, St. Peter's Church in Rome. To get the necessary funds the irreligious pope encouraged the wholesale distribution of indulgences, which were tokens of remitted penalty for sins. The theology of indulgences is complicated and the superstitious and gullible people interpreted them as purchasable tickets of release of their loved ones from purgatory.

One John Tetzel sold these freely near Luther's town, and fired the reformer's religious passion.

Thus awakened, Luther posted on the door of the University of Wittenberg—following an existing practice of the day—a series of 95 theses or sentences that he proposed to debate. These obviously indicated his drift from the Roman Catholic Church.

The priesthood, he taught, was not limited to a few but spread to all believers. The priests could not hinder anyone from reaching God. Each man himself stood before God without the need for priestly intercession or sacrifice. Neither popes nor councils were free from error.

Such teaching soon brought the wrath of the pope, and in 1520 Luther was served notice that he had 60 days to withdraw his opinions. Disregarding the notice, Luther burned it publicly amid the cheers of his students at the university. The next year, the pope excommunicated him from the church and the break was complete.

Luther's Influence

In what ways was the forceful leadership and religious zeal of Luther to stamp all subsequent history?

1. *He initiated Protestantism.* For this he will always be remembered. The personal struggles of his own soul, satisfied with the glorious discovery that salvation is personal and comes from faith in Christ's righteousness, expressed the longings of many persons before and since.

2. *He began Lutheranism.* The denomination that bears his name was not Luther's goal but was the product of his work. Lutheranism became the established form of Protestantism in Germany. It soon

spread northward to the Scandinavian countries. Denmark, Norway, Sweden—are all predominantly Lutheran in name if not wholly in spirit.

3. *He translated the German Bible.* Luther put the New Testament into the language of the German people in the amazing time of 11 weeks. Following his condemnation and while he was in danger, friends kidnapped him and a sympathetic ruler sheltered him for over 1 year in a castle. There Luther busied himself with translating and writing. The translation of the Bible he produced (he completed the Old Testament later) did much to standardize the German language in suceeding centuries.

4. *He reformed Germany.* Although religious wars and turmoil followed his bold break with Rome, within a generation he had secured the religious remaking of Germany and brought about a peace that permitted Protestantism.

> In closing this account of Luther and the momentous movement which he set rolling, we might append an ironic footnote to history. The same sale of indulgences which furnished money to build a fitting capital for a universal Church (St. Peter's in Rome) provided at the same time the occasion for destroying the Church's unchallenged position (Wallbank and Taylor, *Civilization Past and Present* [Chicago: Scott Foresman, 1960], 4th ed., vol. I, p. 475).

Huldreich Zwingli and Switzerland

During this time Switzerland was a federation of 13 small states called "cantons." In one of them just 52 days after Luther was born, Huldreich Zwingli was born. Under Zwingli, as under Luther, reformation arose.

After sound training in the new spirit of education of the day, Zwingli took charge of a small Swiss parish. In the following years he developed evangelical ideas. He borrowed a copy of the first published Greek New Testament that was put out in 1516 and copied the epistles of Paul by hand before returning the book. Many readings of these precious manuscripts formed right religious ideas in his mind.

The Revival in Learning, as it is called, assisted in the promotion of Protestant ideas. For the leaders could now read the Scriptures themselves.

In 1519 Zwingli's reputation as a preacher brought him to one of Switzerland's leading cities, Zurich. There he became seriously ill. As a result, his faith deepened and he boldly published his ideas. So widespread became his disturbing influence that a council was called to examine him. But Zwingli and his gospel of reform won and the council favored him. One by one, with increasing momentum, the cantons of Switzerland began to reform.

Differences With Luther

While Luther and Zwingli alike opposed the corruption of the papacy and the general decay of religion, there were important differences between them. These may perhaps be traced in part to a primary difference in education. Luther was schooled in the traditional learning of the Middle Ages. Zwingli was trained under the leading proponents of the new learning ushered in by the Renaissance. Thus, Zwingli was more open to change than Luther.

Luther believed there was some sacramental effect in baptism; that it had something to do with regeneration. Zwingli taught that it merely symbolized entrance into the Christian community. Luther believed in the "real presence" of Christ in the elements of wine and bread. Zwingli taught that these were only memorials.

One of the peaks of reform under Zwingli was

when in 1525 he announced and conducted a Communion service in lieu of the Mass. Another difference appeared in Zwingli's lack of a critical religious experience, as Luther had undergone. Zwingli's experience came later in the form of illness.

Though a definite attempt at union was made, Luther refused to enter into a league with Zwingli on the basis of Zwingli's disagreement with him. This marks the beginning of legitimate division in Protestantism, a feature to be expected within a movement teaching that every man himself stands before God and the Word of God. Zwingli was the first of several important men who formed what has come to be known as the "Reformed" wing of Protestantism. The Lutheran and the Reformed were the earliest branches of the Protestant movement.

John Calvin and France

Few more brilliant men have been consecrated to the service of God than John Calvin. The son of well-placed French parents, Calvin was always a cultured gentleman. At 14 in Paris he began studies for the priesthood. Some years later he turned to the study of law, which was the wish of his lawyer father. After his father died in 1531, Calvin concentrated on making himself a scholar.

Just how Calvin became a Protestant is unknown. But it is generally believed he came under the influence of Luther's writings. Born in 1509—26 years after Luther—Calvin was part of the second generation of Protestant reformers. By 1533 he was declared a Protestant in his native France and had to flee the persecution against Protestants in that land. He went to Switzerland, never returning to France after the age of 27.

For several years Calvin stayed in Switzerland,

uncertain of the course he should take. In 1536, at the age of 26, he published the first edition of a doctrinal treatise on Protestant theology. Titled *The Institutes of the Christian Religion,* this book was gradually expanded and enlarged. It is universally recognized as one of the finest and most influential books on systematic theology ever written.

While Luther started with the priesthood of believers, Calvin began with the sovereignty of God. This led him to his doctrine of predestination which has characterized the Reformed wing of Protestantism.

Calvin's influence radiated from the city of Geneva in Switzerland. He made this city a model community, linking civil and ecclesiastical rule. Calvin's influence also spread to Scotland and England through the training school he set up in Geneva.

John Knox and Scotland

The state of the clergy in Scotland during the 16th century was notoriously low. The better citizens wished and worked for the overthrow of such corruption.

Through association with other Protestants (including some Scots burned for their faith) and a time in Geneva under Calvin, John Knox was fired with the zeal of evangelical religion. About 1560 Knox and the Scottish Parliament declared that country free from the domination of the pope, declared the Mass illegal, and accepted a strongly Calvinistic confession of faith.

Once it became Protestant, the Scottish church faced the possibility of becoming episcopal. English rulers attempted to force on the young church an organization including bishops. But the Scottish church shied away from this and after some time the presbyterian system of elders, who review both minister and people, was instituted. Thus today both English and Scottish churches are Protestant, but the English church is episcopal and the Scottish church is presbyterian.

12

The Early Modern Church

The 20th century lies cradled in the years from 1650 to 1900. During this time nations were formed, ideas were tested, and discoveries were made that matured during the century in which we live.

The Thirty Years' War was fought for religious reasons. Many of the small rulers of Europe were involved. There was widespread disagreement about who owned what land, in view of the claims of the Roman Catholic Church. When the Thirty Years' War (1618-1648) ended, France emerged as the most powerful European state. Persecution ended.

The fortunes of France were tied in with the history of the Roman Catholic Church. Seventeenth-century France was prosperous and productive. It was in this century, from 1661 to 1715, that the pompous monarch Louis XIV reigned.

Louis XIV operated on the undoubted assumption that kings ruled by the will of God. He argued the "divine right of kings." Nothing could be too good for this majestic prince. Discontent with the suitable facilities used by the French kings before him, Louis XIV ordered the famous extravagant palace of Versailles to be constructed on a marsh several miles from Paris. A hundred million dollars was expended to make this the royal showplace of Europe. As many as 30,000 men labored on the project at one time. To this unsurpassably beautiful palace done in

Italian baroque style came the royalty of Europe. The palace typified the man and the times in France.

The next century in France brought the horrible French Revolution. The times bred revolution. The American Revolution occurred between 1775 and 1783, with the adoption of the Constitution in 1789. Beyond this era of history the rights of the individual were asserted and the institution of the king trended downward.

Individual rights were asserted in philosophy as well. It was the "age of reason." Man wanted to think for himself. The church could no longer tell him what to believe.

In the medieval period the church was the unquestioned superior authority. With the arrival of the Reformation, Christians dethroned the church and elevated the Bible to its rightful place. Followers of the Renaissance accepted neither the Bible nor the church but relied solely on their own reason.

It was an age of imperialism; when the European states reached out to the far corners of newly discovered worlds and created colonies. Commerce expanded to these virgin shores. The merchants, jealous of their profits, strongly opposed the earliest attempts at Christian missions.

Canada became a dominion in the British Empire in 1867. Australia joined in 1901.

America thrived in the early years of the 19th century, coming to a tragic Civil War in 1861 to 1865.

Railroads crossed the United States in 1869. The steamship made its first voyage in 1807, but steam power had been applied to industry as early as the late 1700's. In 1815 macadam roads were first used. It was an era of great canals: the Erie in 1825, the Suez in 1869, and the Panama in 1914.

Morse invented the telegraph in 1844. Faraday invented the first electric dynamo in 1831. Before the century was over, Edison gave the incandescent light and the phonograph and Bell gave the telephone. It was indeed a great age.

Christianity in France

1. *Seventeenth-century Catholicism.* The Reformation century, the 16th, did not find France in a healthy condition. The Reformed or Calvinistic Protestants there were a tiny minority. Toward the end of that century, however, the glory of France began to return. By the reign of "The Grand Monarch," Louis XIV, France flowered.

Two forms of Roman Catholicism appeared during this time. The one advocated patriotism as well as Catholicism. The other urged total commitment to the pope, even at the expense of patriotism.

2. *Persecution of the Protestants.* A most virile group of Protestants in France was the group known as the Huguenots. Unlike the majority of people in the Reformation, these were men of position and wealth. They were a talented stock, not easily willing to give up their faith. In 1598 a decree called the "Edict of Nantes" guaranteed the Huguenots freedom of worship. But during the reign of Louis XIV the edict was reversed. The king sought total uniformity to his reign and the freedom of this significant people seemed to threaten his sovereignty. He was not motivated by allegiance to the pope and the Roman Catholic Church.

The reversal of the Edict of Nantes forced the Huguenots to flee from their native land. Historians reckon this loss as beyond repair. They estimate about 400,000 Huguenots left France, in spite of severe penalties inflicted for leaving the country. "Thousands of her best citizens were put to death or broken in body by torture and imprisonment. . . .

Even worse was the moral loss to France—a loss which has never been made good" (Robert H. Nichols, *The Growth of the Christian Church* [Philadelphia: Westminster, 1941], pp. 250, 251). Here is another example of national failure based on resistance to the people of God.

3. *Nineteenth-century Catholicism.* When the French Revolution came about in 1789, the Catholic Church was stripped of much of its property. Its monastic orders were destroyed. This rebellion was against religion in any form, except the "religion" of reason; and in 1793 Christian worship was forbidden, although it was restored 2 years later.

Napoleon came to power, a self-seeking, vain man. His actions embarrassed the pope. Violating a treaty he had made with the pope, the eccentric French general sent troops to Rome and even held the pope prisoner for a time. Following Napoleon's defeat at Waterloo, Pope Pius VIII reestablished the lands owned by the church in the central area of Italy. After an Italian conqueror took these states from the pope in the year 1870, the pope refused to leave the Vatican lest he seem to recognize his conquerors. The pope remained inside the Vatican palace, a voluntary prisoner.

Other developments in Catholicism are of more importance. In 1870 at the first general council called since Reformation days, the pope was declared to be infallible when speaking about doctrinal matters. This does not mean the pope cannot make any error whatsoever, but it assures the faithful that when he speaks officially in matters of doctrine he cannot err. The vote which gave him this right was 533 to 2. Some years before, in 1854, the doctrine of the Immaculate Conception of the Virgin Mary was announced by the pope. It declared that the mother of Jesus was not conceived in sin. This pronouncement continued the Roman development of the doctrine of Mary.

Developments in England

1. *Puritanism.* In the years following the English Reformation, some Christians in England became discontent with the extent to which reforms had been made. Courageous men of high character and severe moral standards, they wanted further "purifying" of the Church of England. They wished to do away with all traces of Romanism, like the cross still remaining on the altars of English churches, the vestments used by the clergy, and certain ceremonial rites. Because of their desire to purify, these people were called Puritans.

Soon the Puritans gained an important position in government, where they could wield their influence. They succeeded in gaining enough control of the Church to change for a time its government, from the episcopal bishops to the presbyterian elders which more suited their Calvinistic tastes. This change did not last, however, and the Church of England was restored to the episcopal type of government.

But the Puritans did succeed in persuading King James to authorize a new translation of the Bible, which was then named after him. They produced in the Westminster Assembly (a convention called to plot the reformation of the Church of England) the Westminster Catechisms, both the larger and the shorter, which are widely known and used.

2. *Wesleyanism.* Eighteenth-century England forsook the influence forced on it by the Puritans several generations earlier. As if in spite of Puritan standards, widespread immorality generated an

overall low point in English history. To this scene came John Wesley, born in 1703.

Wesley was a distinguished scholar of Oxford University. There he, his brother Charles, and a friend, George Whitefield, assembled in, what were called in jest, "Holy Clubs." Wesley was a disciplined Christian, and with the methodical stewardship of time which the "Holy Club" practiced, the name *Methodist* originated.

In an early mission to Georgia he failed and returned to England. From there, however, he directed the formation of the Methodist Church in America. He was not the first servant of Christ who learned from failure at the beginning of his ministry.

During his lifetime, Wesley is said to have preached more than 40,000 sermons, traveling up to 5,000 miles a year and preaching wherever he could. He gave the world the Methodist Church, stirred England to a deep revival of true religion, initiated Christian social service, and sparked the revival of Christian missions.

Pietism in Germany

One of the unfortunate chapters of Church history is the state of religion in Germany in the years subsequent to the days of Luther. The Lutheran Church had become spiritually cold. It concerned itself with right belief more than right experience. So long as one assented to the correct religious doctrines, he was right with God. Consequently, it was a period of heavy theological controversy. Some accord was reached with the *Formula of Concord,* an elaborate statement of faith set forth in 1577. The *Formula* came to be viewed as defining the total content of Christian doctrine, and it became the basis for the theological preaching of the time, which did not effectively reach the people.

Seeking the restoration of faith and life in personal religion, the movement known as Pietism appeared within Lutheranism during the 17th and 18th centuries.

Much influence in the Pietistic movement was wielded by Philip Jacob Spener (1635-1705). He wrote a book titled *Pius Longings*. He also instituted cottage prayer meetings and greatly encouraged the study of the Bible and the development of personal spirituality. August Francke (1663-1727) became a friend of Spener, and Spener helped Francke secure a position as a professor in the University of Halle.

Through the Pietistic influence, modern Christian missions were stimulated. A German Pietist pastor in New Jersey was instrumental in the life of Gilbert Tennant, one of the preachers in the American Great Awakening of Jonathan Edward's day.

Pietism shows that when the fires of an original revival movement die down, there is likely to arise a group who will once again emphasize personal religion and fresh Bible study.

The Rebirth of Missions

The Reformation, it has been pointed out by historians, was not a missionary movement. It was concerned primarily with internal church reform. It was, so to speak, the church pulling the mote out of its own eye before attempting to remove beams from the eyes of the heathen.

1. *Von Welz, the "missionary agitator."* In 1664 in a series of pamphlets, this man, a member of the Austrian nobility, began probing the church with challenging questions. He asked whether it was

right for Christians to keep the gospel to themselves and not seek to share it with other nations. Is it right, he queried, not to challenge theological students to spread the gospel to other lands? And could Christians afford, in the light of eternal values, to spend so much on unnecessary luxuries when much of the world needed the gospel? Meeting great opposition, Von Welz nevertheless awakened many to their missionary obligation.

2. *The first mission.* This honor belongs to the Pietists from the University of Halle. The King of Denmark, King Frederick IV, had been shown the need of Christianizing people in the Danish colonies. Two men from Halle, under appointment of the good king, went accordingly to India, leaving in 1705. Facing insurmountable obstacles, within 2 years they had learned the language and baptized both Danish slaves and Hindu converts.

3. *Count von Zinzendorf.* Brought up under Pietist influence and trained first at Halle then at the University of Wittenberg, this nobleman became a bishop among the Moravians, a group of Christians originating even before the Reformation broke out. At his wedding altar he was led to renounce his noble position, surrender his property, and consecrate his life to the service of Christ.

Once, while at a meeting, he saw two Eskimos from Greenland and a Negro from the West Indies. Much impressed, he returned to his church to lay down a challenge to propagate the gospel. Hearing of this, his church agreed to take up the work in Greenland which was about to be given up. They also spread the gospel to Central and South America, Alaska, South Africa, Australia, and to the American Indians. The Count lived by his motto: "I have one passion: it is He and He alone."

4. *William Carey.* Called "the father of modern missions," William Carey (1761-1834) labored as a shoemaker to support himself while he pastored a church offering a meager salary. Before him in the shoeshop he kept a world map. As he repaired shoes, he prayed. In his spare time he read and studied, mastering Latin, Greek, Hebrew, Dutch, and even botany and zoology—thereby preparing himself to become the first missionary sent by the first Baptist Missionary Society of England. Carey went to India. His influence opened up the whole modern period of missions.

American Revivalism

Rising from a wilderness to the leading world power in 300 years, America developed as a Christian nation. Revivalism followed its westward-pushing frontier and wove Christianity into the American fabric. Here is a brief glance at the major revivals prior to the 20th century.

1. *The Great Awakening.* In the Colonial era, French doubt had affected the early Americans and religious decay was apparent. Between 1734 and 1742 a spirited revival came to the colonies. Starting in the middle colonies among the Irish Presbyterians, it moved north to the Congregationalists under Jonathan Edwards, then southward to the Episcopalians. Besides yielding a large number of converts, the Great Awakening restored a Christian perspective to the country that was about to be born by revolution.

2. *The Great Revival.* The year 1800 found the infant nation creeping westward. Leaving behind the moral control of the cities, the rugged pioneers settled in temporary camps where neither policemen nor clergymen were to be found. Morals went

unchecked. In the eastern cities, students sold out to the "age of reason." The revival came in two phases that were about as opposite as they could be. President Timothy Dwight of Yale publicly discussed theology and effected the conversion of many students. In the Kentucky wilderness, Peter Cartwright and others began the camp meetings where thousands of common folk met Christ.

3. *The prayer-meeting revival.* Nearly the emotional opposite of the Kentucky revival, the Fulton Street prayer meeting of 1857-58 quietly brought 100,000 people into the church within 4 months. It began with a layman, Jeremiah Lanphier, who invited businessmen into the North Dutch Church in New York City to pray. Their prayers brought a stirring revival.

13

The Twentieth Century

No century matches the 20th for scientific advancements. Built on the preceding years when scientific studies multiplied after the revival of learning, these decades have compressed an unbelievable quantity of events into a very short and ominous period.

Everywhere now the question is survival. With all the scientific advances, with all the increasing supply of leisure devices and time, there comes also the probing question: Will man survive? The startling fact is that the leaps of progress made in communication, transportation, manufacturing, and such areas have not been accompanied by a corresponding advance in morals. On the contrary, it seems the more enriched life has become through the gifts of science, the deeper has become human sinfulness. While science shoots upward, sin plummets downward.

This is the major truth of the 20th century: Man now stands with the possibility of destroying himself from the face of the earth. Not till the mid-20th century was this possible. We caught a frightful vision of it when in 1945 a single atomic bomb leveled the city of Hiroshima.

Such talk is not mere chatter. Statesmen, novelists, philosophers, artists, professors, and clergymen all recognize the awful power of self-destruction now in the hands of the human race. Pessimism and despair are on every hand—and rightly so.

But the humble Christian is the one who has hope. While others worry about the destruction of the body, he rests in the assurance of the salvation of the soul and the resurrection of the body.

The 20th-century World

When the 20th century opened, all was optimistic. America had come out of its Civil War through Reconstruction days with a grand switch toward industrialization. Mass production methods gave the title "Second Industrial Revolution" to the years 1870 to 1914.

Promising inventions and discoveries yielded optimistic expectations. As the century opened, wireless telegraphy spanned the ocean. The Wright brothers floated through the air at Kitty Hawk. Henry Ford designed a low-priced carriage that would run by itself. The discovery of X rays and radium added to earlier discoveries of anesthetics, and a new age was born in medicine.

Louis Sullivan brought in the skyscraper, and one of his pupils, Frank Lloyd Wright, designed houses that seemed to grow out of the land on which they were erected.

New York, with 700,000 people in 1850, had more than 3 million a half century later. It was the age of the city; people moved from farms to the newly created jobs in urban areas.

All these inventions and discoveries had the effect of shrinking the world. Man was growing, both culturally and numerically, but the world was shrinking and people were gaining international interests.

When the clouds of war gathered in 1914, it was a fearsome sight. The war was of such magnitude it was correctly called a World War. The major powers of the Western world were at odds with each other. The clash brought on new and fearful methods of war. Under the guise of developing water tanks, Britain produced the war tank that terrified the German soldiers. Poisonous gases were released that had fatal or crippling effects.

It was hailed as the war to end wars, and great jubilation followed the armistice signed in 1918. The next year the League of Nations was formed, and hopes for peace were high.

Yet within another generation came still another global war, and historians began numbering them; this was World War II. If the first produced its fearful weapons, the second outdid it. The skies were filled with fighting planes far more destructive than the earlier ones of World War I.

A turning point in history arrived with the bombing of Hiroshima. "As the mushroom-shaped cloud rose over the city, only charred ruins were left beneath; an expanse of approximately 3 miles square—about 60 percent of the city—was almost completely obliterated. The Japanese government estimated that 60,000 people died, 100,000 were wounded, and 200,000 were left homeless" (Walter Wallbank et al, *Civilization Past and Present* [Glenview, IL: Scott, Foresman & Co., 1960 ed.], Vol. II, p. 558).

Between the wars, severe depression had ravaged America, forcing many out of their homes and businesses. While this happened in America, a cruel and misguided dictator had risen in Germany. His drive for power left behind a path of inhuman atrocities that staggered even the 20-century imagination. Not less than 6 million Jews were killed. People rubbed their eyes; could this happen in the midst of such a golden era of achievement?

It could happen. And it did. As man's capacity to control his world expanded, so did his capacity to do evil. To such a world speaks the Church of this century.

Liberalism

One of the intellectual trends in the 20th century is theological liberalism. Liberalism is similar to modernism, although some say there are slight differences between them. Both words describe low views of the Bible and of the miraculous elements of religion in particular.

1. *Modernism began with exchanging human reason for the Bible.* If the Bible says Jesus walked on water, those who accept its authority will not question that He did. But those who trust their own judgment over the Bible will test its statements by their own reason. Since a miracle is unreasonable and contrary to the ordinary course of nature, it must not be believed. If evolution says man and animal have a common ancestor, the Bible must be wrong.

2. *Modernistic preaching turned toward collective social action at the expense of personal religious salvation.* This is called the "social gospel." The work of the church became identified with the clearance of slum areas, the education of neglected persons, the elevation of literacy, and various types of social work. Now none of these, from a Biblical standpoint, should be neglected. But the error was that the reality of sin and the need for personal repentance and forgiveness were often no part of the message.

3. *The great doctrines of Christianity recovered in the Reformation were neglected.* Man was no longer a sinner, according to the modernists. Sin was a bad example, not an inward reality. Blood atone-

ment was too brutal to be accepted. The Bible was inspired in the same sense as Shakespeare's works were. Christ was a man, the most perfect man, but His divinity was something that would not demand the Virgin Birth or a literal resurrection.

4. *This modernistic gospel was strongly challenged in 1920.* The challenge was represented by three distinct movements not related to each other. They were neoorthodoxy, Fundamentalism, and Pentecostalism.

5. *Karl Barth, a Swiss pastor and professor, initiated "neoorthodoxy."* In a commentary on the Book of Romans, he whipped the modernists for overlooking the basically sinful nature of man. Barth had World War I to prove it; did not man manifest his evil heart in this global struggle? The modernists were greatly embarrassed by the war that had shattered their rosy optimism. Barth's criticisms stung. Moving away from modernism and back toward Biblical theology, Barth's views were called "neoorthodox" because they represented a new drift toward the orthodox teaching of Christianity.

Fundamentalism

1. *An important reaction against modernism was Fundamentalism.* The name came from a series of free pamphlets sent out by the millions in the years following 1910. They were titled *The Fundamentals*. Sponsored by two Christian laymen and guided by a committee of ministers, various Bible-believing scholars wrote understandable articles setting forth the five fundamental doctrines that needed emphasis at the time. These were: (1) the inerrancy of the Scriptures; (2) the virgin birth of Christ; (3) His physical resurrection; (4) His substitutionary atonement by blood; and (5) His second coming.

The pamphlets were mailed to every available address of Sunday school teachers and superintendents, pastors, teachers in colleges and schools, YMCA secretaries, and other religious personnel. They brought to the attention of the American public the long-cherished doctrines of Christianity which had been challenged by the modernists.

2. *Fundamentalism gained nationwide attention during the famous "Scopes Trial" in 1925.* John T. Scopes had taught evolution in the schools of Tennessee. This was contrary to a law passed a few months earlier. The famous orator, William Jennings Bryan, prosecuted the defendant and the well-known criminal lawyer Clarence Darrow defended him. The outcome of the trial saw Scopes convicted and fined, but the effect of the trial was to make a national issue over the Bible versus evolution.

3. *Several new denominations resulted from the controversy.* This happened as the Bible believers were unsuccessful in ridding their denominations of modernism and were forced out. For example, J. Gresham Machen, a staunch Presbyterian professor at Princeton Seminary, founded Westminster Seminary and the Orthodox Presbyterian Church. Similar splits occurred in Baptist churches and elsewhere.

4. *About 1950 a group of "New Evangelicals" arose within Fundamentalism.* These men felt Fundamentalism had become negative and defensive and its best service had been done some years before. They were alert to the new challenge presented by Karl Barth and wished to oppose neoorthodoxy without being negative. When this happened some of the older Fundamentalists took the name Ultra-fundamentalist, or even Ultra-ultra-fundamentalist. From about mid-century, Fundamentalism was thus divided.

Pentecostalism

1. *Another movement that opposed modernism was Pentecostalism.* Unlike Fundamentalism, the Pentecostal movement did not begin in protest against the theological drift in the modernist churches. Instead, it began with deep spiritual hunger. Thirst for spiritual reality was more predominant among early Pentecostals than was indignation over departure from orthodoxy.

2. *The deep spiritual hunger of many was satisfied with the outpouring of the Holy Spirit at the opening of the century.* On January 1, 1901 in a small Kansas Bible school, the first known person in modern times received the baptism in the Holy Spirit in answer to definite prayer. Within several years, others throughout the country and in other parts of the world witnessed the arrival of the Spirit.

3. *In 1914 a call went out that resulted in the formation of the General Council of the Assemblies of God, one of the leading classical Pentecostal churches.* This is the same year World War I began. After the initial outpouring of the Holy Spirit, a number of Pentecostal churches were formed.

Persons receiving the Holy Spirit often wished to return to their churches but in many cases they were not permitted to do so. The meetings at Azusa Street in Los Angeles, California had triggered a round-the-world Pentecostal movement. Many ministers visited the meetings there and carried the Pentecostal message to their distant congregations. It was decided to band together in a voluntary fellowship for the best interests of all. Other Pentecostal denominations were formed for various reasons.

4. *The Pentecostal movement was primarily revivalistic and evangelistic.* It was not concerned at first with theology or education. The early Pentecos-

tals already had both. Their main concern was renewed preaching of the gospel in the power of the Holy Spirit, who had entered the believers' experience in a new way. There was no heresy combated, no previously existing denomination fought. Simply a new dimension of spiritual reality had been found and was being shared.

The first Pentecostal schools were Bible schools, designed to train ministers and missionaries who would spread the good news. Only in 1955 was Evangel College, a Christian liberal arts college, founded by Pentecostals.

5. *Pentecostalism is not the same thing as Fundamentalism.* There are similarities, but there are also important differences. Doctrinally, Pentecostals align closely with Fundamentalists, but Pentecostals are more concerned with experience than with doctrine. This does not mean they in any way belittle doctrine. It means they assume Biblical orthodoxy and go on from there to a heartwarming personal experience. In this respect they resemble the 17th-century Lutheran Pietists.

6. *The witness of the Pentecostal movement began to spread to other denominations about mid-century.* The Pentecostal movement grew and flourished as one of the fastest-growing movements in Christianity. By 1960 over 5 million Pentecostals could be counted throughout the world. Then many in other denominations began receiving the baptism in the Holy Spirit without, however, coming into the Pentecostal movement. This led to the emergence of the charismatic movement.

Ecumenism

1. *The 20th century saw increasing agitation for the achievement of one church.* Protestant sec-

tarianism was a source of embarrassment to all. Jesus had prayed "that they may be one" (John 17:22).

2. *This ecumenical movement began in the last century with interdenominational cooperation.* The founding of Bible societies, such as the American Bible Society in 1816, brought about the collective effort of several denominations.

3. *The next stage was organic reunion.* On numerous occasions denominations have joined together into one large denomination. The Methodist Church, for example, had divided in the Civil War days, but they reunited in 1939. Congregationalists, Methodists, and Presbyterians merged in 1925 into the United Church of Canada. In the 1950's this trend increased. The Evangelical and Reformed Church united with the Congregational Christian Church to form the United Church of Christ. The Unitarians and the Universalists began to merge. Similar unions and plans for unions were under way elsewhere.

4. *The 4th stage was the formation of national and international federations of denominations.* In 1908 the Federal Council of Churches of Christ in America was formed, having some 30 member denominations. In 1950 this organization united with some other missionary and educational organizations to form the National Council of Churches (NCC).

Two major church councils arose composed of Bible-believing, or conservative, Christian churches. The American Council of Christian Churches (ACC), founded in 1941, takes a very hostile approach to the NCC and is its most ardent critic. The major counterpart to the NCC is the National Association of Evangelicals (NAE). Founded in 1943, it will admit as members individuals or churches whose denominations are members of the

NCC. The NAE is more moderate in its methods though it is no less critical of the theological inadequacy of the NCC.

5. *The ecumenical movement finds its highest expression in the World Council of Churches (WCC).* Created formally in Amsterdam in 1948, this international council brought together many groups and national councils. WCC is criticized by some evangelicals because of its lack of an adequate theological platform.

6. *True church union is the one that already exists.* This seems clear from the Biblical teaching regarding the invisible Church. The ecumenical movement may be accused of seeking outward unity at the expense of inner, theological agreement. While it may not be wrong to cooperate with larger councils for certain purposes, it appears unwise to enter full association as long as the doctrinal basis is so flexible.

Only time will tell what will be the earthly future of the Church. But its destiny is assured: against it, the gates of hell shall not prevail.

Suggestions for Further Reading

While it is difficult to name a single book on the doctrine of the Church that does not reflect a particular viewpoint, Lesslie Newbigin's older work *The Household of God* (New York: Friendship Press, 1954) ingeniously outlines the Protestant, Catholic, and Pentecostal approaches to the Christian community. Frank Mead's *Handbook of Denominations* (Nashville: Abingdon, 6th ed., 1975) neatly summarizes the history, beliefs, and statistics of the American churches.

Why not read Church history in the light of its missionary expansion? The story is told with competence and style in *A History of the Expansion of Christianity* (Grand Rapids: Zondervan Publishing House, 1970) by Kenneth S. Latourette. The extensive booklists in these seven inexpensive paperback volumes provide a lifetime of reading on the life and leaders of the Church.